THOMAS GORDON SMITH

Construction of Ionic order
(monochrome wash drawing)

NAMONOGRAPH

THOMAS GORDON SMITH

AND THE REBIRTH OF CLASSICAL ARCHITECTURE

Richard John

opposite:
Vitruvian House, South Bend, Portico

above:
Sunnyside, Wisconcin

ANDREAS **PAPADAKIS** PUBLISHER

Cover:
Civic Center, Cathedral City, view of entrance on axis

PUBLISHER'S NOTE
NA Monographs continues an idea we developed many years ago to publish in monographic form the work of important international architects. I am especially pleased to publish in this volume, the third of the new series, the work of the distinguished academic and leading architect Thomas Gordon Smith whose vision broadens the barriers of classical architecture.

Designed by Vicky Braouzou

First published in Great Britain by ANDREAS PAPADAKIS PUBLISHER
An imprint of New Architecture Group Limited
16 Grosvenor Place, London SW1X 7HH, United Kingdom

ISBN 1 901092 21 6

Printed and bound in Singapore

CONTENTS

above:
St Joseph Catholic Church, Dalton, Georgia

opposite:
Richmond Hill House, Richmond, exterior view at dusk

INTRODUCTION

For the last two decades, Thomas Gordon Smith has played a central role in the revival of classicism in contemporary architecture in America. In the late 1970s he became a key figure in the development of Post-Modernism but after contributing to that movement's seminal exhibition at the Venice Biennale in 1980 he rejected the ironical approach of Robert Venturi and the decontextualization of Charles Moore, to develop an architecture which draws freely on the twenty-five centuries of the classical tradition. His conviction in the enduring relevance of this tradition to contemporary life has resulted in buildings which in terms of materials and function are just as much a product of the modern world as a high tech office building or a Deconstructionist museum extension; however, in addition to admirably fulfilling the job for which they were intended, his buildings also have the rare quality of engaging us intellectually, rooting us historically and uplifting us spiritually.

Smith grew up in the San Francisco Bay Area of Northern California, far from the "high" classicism of that East Coast tradition which extends from Thomas Jefferson to John Russell Pope; instead, his earliest and perhaps most profound influence was Bernard Maybeck, the Beaux Arts trained craftsman-architect who fused a wide-ranging knowledge of architectural history and a fascination with modern materials and techniques in highly idiosyncratic buildings. As we shall see, Smith has come to pursue a similar synthesis in his own work.

This book will present for the first time all of Smith's buildings and projects. It will also explore the polymathic range of his other activities, including his influential role as an educator, commentator on Vitruvius, historian of the Greek Revival, painter of frescoes, and designer and collector of furniture.

The subtitle of this volume "The Rebirth of Classical Architecture" is not intended to suggest that Smith alone is responsible for the success of the modern classical movement. Clearly, a number of his contemporaries have made equally influential contributions; however, almost all of these individuals developed their ideas in isolation, each pursuing a trajectory which came to form part of the overall movement. It is this individual story which I believe deserves to be told.

I should like here to record my gratitude to Anthony Bruce and Leslie Emmington Jones of the Berkeley Architectural Heritage Association. In the summer of 1997 they kindly enabled me to see numerous buildings in Berkeley, including the Temple of the Wings and a number of Maybeck houses, which had an impact on Thomas Gordon Smith in his youth. I should also like to thank my publisher Dr Andreas Papadakis for his encouragement of this project and Dr David Watkin for his support.

Finally, I owe an immense debt of gratitude to Thomas Gordon Smith and his wife, Marika, not just for their cooperation on this book, but also for their friendship in recent years.

Bernard Maybeck and A. Randolph Monro, the Temple of the Wings, Berkeley, Ca.
Photograph of Florence Boynton and her children

CHAPTER I

Early Influences and Education

"So you want to be an applied archaeologist?"
Claude Stoller

Thomas Gordon Smith was born in Oakland, California, in 1948. His mother Margaret was an artist who painted abstract landscapes, and his father Sheldon was an academic historian. When he was five the family moved to El Cerrito, a small suburban city a short distance East along the San Francisco Bay from Oakland and Berkeley. In the 1930s this city had acquired a reputation for fast living, with a greyhound racetrack and numerous brothels and gambling dens. During the post-war period, however, a reforming city council thoroughly cleaned El Cerrito up, purging it of vice to create "a city of homes" in place of the "little Reno" which had existed before.[1]

As a child, Smith used to escape from the stultifying suburban enclave of El Cerrito to the excitement of neighbouring Berkeley. Here one could still experience the spirit of intellectual freedom which had earned the city the alias "Athens of the West" and had inspired the eclectic Arts and Crafts architect Bernard Maybeck. This spirit found its epitome in one early Berkeley inhabitant, Florence Treadwell Boynton, a disciple of Isadora Duncan who dressed her children in the *Stola* and *Pallium* of the ancient Greeks.[2] She raised them, appropriately enough, in a house which she had designed with Maybeck in 1911 in the form of a classical peristyle open to the elements. Known as the Temple of the Wings, from the curved shape of its roof, this extraordinary structure consisted of thirty-four giant concrete Corinthian columns and was perched high

up in the Berkeley hills with a view out to the Golden Gate of the San Francisco Bay. Following its near destruction by fire in 1923, proper walls were built between the columns to replace the tarps which originally had been the only means of enclosure. In the 1960s a neighbourhood dancing school was still being held at the house, preserving a memory of its earliest residents and their bohemian lifestyle. Seeing this bizarre house and learning of its romantic associations inspired Smith at the age of fourteen to be an architect.[3]

The beginning of his undergraduate career coincided with a sabbatical for his father in Europe and so in 1966 Smith spent his first year at university enrolled at the American College in Paris. Since the University of California at Berkeley did not accept entrants in the Sophomore year, he spent a year at the California State College at Hayward before finally entering Berkeley as a Junior to major in Art. Once there he concentrated mainly on painting, which was taught by Joseph Raphael whose large canvases generally consisted of impressionistic enlargements of natural subjects. Modern dance also occupied much of his time at Berkeley, to the extent that he considered taking a double major, with Drama as his secondary subject. This enthusiasm can be attributed to the inspiring teaching of the former dance master of the Martha Graham Company, David Wood, who had recently arrived with his wife Marnie to teach at Berkeley. Smith was taught by Wood according to the

above:
Thomas and Marika Smith dancing at their wedding

opposite:
Paolo Portoghesi, Casa Baldi. Photograph, TGS

same rigorous training system which Graham herself had developed. This early experience might help to explain the emphasis Smith would later place on processional routes through his buildings, almost as though he was choreographing the spectator.

During his Senior year, Smith was given an opportunity to combine his two interests of dance and architecture when he was awarded a President's fellowship by the university to design and build a dance platform for a hillside setting. Despite this foretaste of an architectural career, however, he began a six-month stint as a baker's apprentice in Oakland shortly after graduating.

In December 1970 he married the nineteen year old Marika Wilson, whose father James, a leading astrophysicist, and Greek-American mother Demetra would later prove to be hugely supportive, in particular by providing Smith with a number of commissions from both themselves and their friends. The following September, the young couple left the United States for what was essentially a belated seven-month honeymoon in Europe. They spent two months in Vicenza, where Smith studied the work of Palladio intensively by visiting his buildings and

reading in the well-stocked library of the Centro internazionale di studi di architettura "Andrea Palladio" then located in the Palazzo Valmarana. A board member of the Centro rented them an apartment during their stay and from this base they visited seventy-five sixteenth- and seventeenth-century villas in the Veneto.

Smith did not restrict his interest to historic buildings while in Italy. Before leaving the United States, he had prepared a detailed guidebook of what he hoped to see and in this he included some illustrations clipped from *Casabella* of recent buildings by Paolo Portoghesi. Knowing that they were near Florence, but not sure exactly where, Smith showed the pictures to an assistant in the tourist information kiosk and asked if she could help him find them. As the works in which Smith was interested were public buildings, the tourist information officer tried looking them up in local directories, but having little success she suggested they do some sightseeing and return later to find out what progress she had made. When they came back they were amazed to discover that, having failed to locate them in any reference books, she had simply called Portoghesi in Rome and asked

where these buildings of his were. The architect, surprised that a young American tourist was so interested in his work, suggested that if Smith and his wife were coming to Rome, he would like to offer them lunch and show them examples of his work there. In due course, therefore, they visited Portoghesi in his penthouse apartment where they found walls covered with William Morris paper and hung with engravings of Borromini's buildings. They ate lunch on the terrace overlooking the gardens of the Villa Medici and afterwards Portoghesi took them to see his Casa Baldi (1961) and Casa Andreas (1965).

Later, Smith would describe how Portoghesi's daring use of Baroque elements in contemporary buildings had a profound impact on him, even though he regretted that the references to Baroque sources were so abstracted.[4] Portoghesi's relationship to the past, however, went deeper than the borrowing of motifs. Portoghesi himself related how, on first entering architecture school, he rapidly realised that those who were supposed to be teaching him "were absolutely unable to do so, [because] they didn't know anything and therefore I kidded myself that I would find a master from several centuries earlier."[5]

Portoghesi thus attempted to forge a pupil-teacher relationship with Borromini as though they were pupil and teacher rather than with any of his university tutors. This type of apprenticeship, to long-dead masters rather than to living practitioners, was to prove a fruitful model for Smith in his own development as an architect.

This extended stay in Italy confirmed Smith in his desire to pursue architecture, and while in Europe he applied to graduate schools. On his return to the United States in March 1972 he visited Princeton University and there met Michael Graves who had been teaching in its school of architecture for the past ten years. Smith's application to Princeton had already been turned down, and Graves encouraged him to apply the following year. This advice proved unnecessary as Smith decided to return to Berkeley where he had been offered a place, noting in a letter to Graves that he thought it was for the best as "there is enough flexibility within the department to insure a freedom for my work as it may develop" and because "the Bay region is the location of a domestic building tradition . . . which has long interested me."[6] Smith was undoubtedly correct in his choice for in the early seventies the architecture school at Berkeley was large and had no required curriculum, while Princeton, on the other hand, could only have offered a much more constraining environment for a student who was genuinely radical in his questioning of the hegemony of modernism.

Once back at Berkeley, Smith rapidly formed a close bond with one of the most distinguished modernists on the faculty of the school of architecture, Joseph Esherick, taking a number of independent studies with him. Esherick, by then in his sixties, had earned widespread acclaim in the 1950s and '60s for his spare updating of the Bay Area style, particularly in his residential work.[7] He was tolerant of Smith's interest in the Prairie style and Palladio, perhaps because he himself had exhibited a certain eclecticism in his work and had notably collaborated with the aged Maybeck in the 1950s.

Another teacher who was enormously supportive of Smith was the historian David Gebhard. Though he was a professor at the University of California at Santa Barbara, Smith chose Gebhard to supervise his thesis on John Hudson Thomas (1878-1945). This Nevada-born architect had grown up in the Bay Area before attending Yale as an undergraduate at the turn of the century. He returned to Berkeley to study architecture under John Galen Howard, remaining there in practice for the rest of his life. Having established his reputation early on with a series of redwood bungalows, his spatially experimental work in the second decade of this century, often in stucco, drew eclectically from a broad range of sources including the Secession movement and the Prairie style. Hudson Thomas abandoned conscious innovation in his later work, which remained individualistic while it increasingly returned to the mediaeval sources underlying the Arts and Crafts movement. In addition to fulfilling the requirements of his degree, Smith's research on Hudson Thomas bore fruit in several other ways: first, the connections he established with the owners of houses by Hudson Thomas led to several commissions to restore, extend or remodel their homes;[8] secondly, he was able to disseminate the findings of his research through lectures and walking tours, before finally publishing an essay on Hudson Thomas in a book on Californian Arts and Crafts architects.[9]

Gebhard had earned a certain notoriety as a critic for his praise of the new Getty Museum in Malibu. This building, designed by Langdon and Wilson Architects with advice from the archaeologist Norman Neuerburg, had been widely criticised for being so closely modelled on the Villa of the Papyri at Pompeii. Given his public sympathies it is not surprising therefore that Gebhard encouraged Smith's enthusiasm for historical precedents. However, he became highly critical when the tribute to the past was too slavish, as in his opinion it was in one studio design project which Smith executed in the Prairie style. In the slim years immediately following Smith's graduation, Gebhard was hugely encouraging: in response to a letter from Smith describing how some of his drawings were being exhibited at the Cooper-Hewitt museum in New York, he urged him "'to get at it' and get something built – I for one would like to see one of your 'creatures' in the real, live world."[10] He would later pay Smith a huge compliment by illustrating the house that Smith built for his family in Richmond, California, on the cover of his popular *Guide to Architecture in San Francisco and Northern California* (1985).[11] Smith, in return, publicly thanked him for having "alerted me to the difference between plagiarism and emulation in architecture."[12]

A rather less supportive faculty member was Professor Claude Stoller (b. 1921) who had trained at Black Mountain College and the Graduate School of Design at Harvard. When, on arrival at Berkeley, Smith explained to Stoller his interest in the architecture of the past, his unsympathetic response was: "So you want to be an applied archaeologist?"[13] This inability to appreciate how history might be relevant to the contemporary design process characterised the attitudes of conventional modernists, and yet the stirrings of post-modernism, which viewed history as a store cupboard to be raided at will, were beginning to be felt.

Dormer and balcony added to John Hudson Thomas house (Zuckerman House)

Detail of new porch and balcony added to an Arts and Crafts cottage, Berkeley

CHAPTER II

First Californian Projects

"I'm striving for a richness of meaning"
Thomas Gordon Smith

During his first summer at architecture school, Smith rehabilitated a cottage in Berkeley for his parents-in-law. This involved designing and constructing an external staircase and a six-bay porch with a balcony above. Although Smith's choice of a salmon coloured paint for the windows and door played a considerable part in revitalising the rather sad-looking shingle cottage, it was his sensitive detailing of the posts and brackets of the porch and the pierced arts and craft panels of the balcony which effected the most dramatic transformation.

Following his graduation in 1975, Smith taught architectural history at the College of Marin, a junior college in Kentfield which offered a two year liberal arts course. Despite his relative youth, Smith was already well prepared for the two survey courses he had to teach which, taken together, essentially covered the entire course of western architecture from primitive structures to the present day. He had begun assembling a collection of architectural slides during his first European trip in 1967 which had taken him to Northern Italy to visit Romanesque churches and also to the French Auvergne and Midi. By the end of 1975, however, the carefully catalogued collection had grown to over 5,000 slides.[1] Before graduating, he had also conducted a number of detailed surveys of historic buildings. In the Fall of 1973 he made axonometric and measured drawings of the second Wallen Maybeck house, which Bernard Maybeck had designed for his son in 1937, and these were subsequently published in the monograph on Maybeck by Kenneth Cardwell in

1977.[2] Since the children of the owners of the house had been friends of his at high school, Smith had known this technologically innovative but stylistically traditional building as a teenager and first sketched it in 1968. His interest in the house stimulated him to design a hypothetical project immediately adjacent to it in 1978, which is described below, and later still he published a scholarly article on the unique methods and materials used in its construction.[3] Smith had his first opportunity to measure a nineteenth-century house when in the summer of 1974 the architect and historian, Kenneth Cardwell recruited him to a team of five draughtsmen to record an adobe house in Monterey which had been built by John Battista Cooper in 1832. Smith went on to spend the rest of the summer working as a draughtsman for the Historic American Buildings Survey in Tennessee, where he helped measure five nineteenth-century buildings, recording them with ink on mylar drawings. One of these was the Samuel Cleage House in Athens, Tennessee, built of brick in about 1825, which had several noteworthy features including stepped gables, moulded brick cornices, and an ornate fanlight.

While teaching at College of Marin Smith sought work in practice, in particular in Joseph Esherick's office, but by now he had already produced his first designs featuring classical columns and while the master himself seemed unconcerned by this development, it was clear that Esherick's partners were disturbed by the prospect of hiring a young radical.

above: Drawing of Bernard Maybeck's Wallen Maybeck House II, 1968

below: Samuel Cleage House, Tennessee, measured drawing

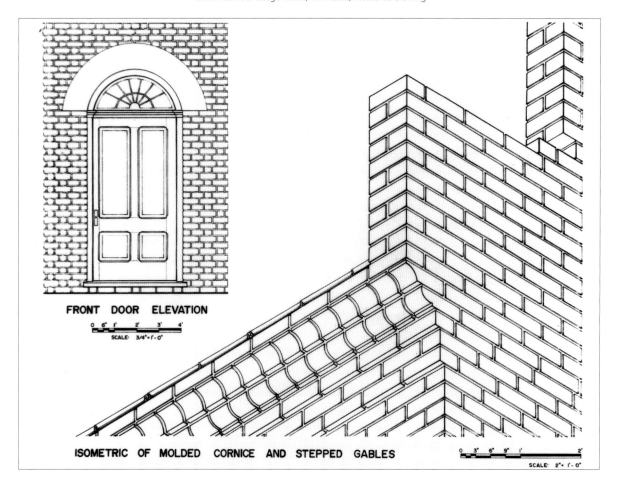

FRONT DOOR ELEVATION

0 6" 1'   2'   3'   4'

SCALE: 3/4"= 1'- 0"

ISOMETRIC OF MOLDED CORNICE AND STEPPED GABLES

0 3" 6" 9" 1'   2'

SCALE: 2"= 1'- 0"

Sunnyside Street House,
Lake Street House, Jefferson Street House
and the Doric House

Doric House, perspective drawing

The designs which Smith produced soon after graduation were for houses for particular sites in the Bay area: Sunnyside Street House, Piedmont; Lake Street House, Piedmont; Jefferson Street House, Berkeley; and the Doric House, Berkeley. All four were intended as possible homes for himself and Marika, taking empty lots as their sites and requiring only modest budgets. After completing the first two, he recorded the three main aims of his design philosophy in these projects as follows: "I have tried to exploit the advantages of views and neighbourhood ambience which older neighbourhoods provide. I have tried to design buildings which will be comfortable in this region's mild climate with a minimal reliance on mechanical heating. Finally, I am attempting to develop a personal image in these houses by integrating and adapting elements from historic and contemporary sources."[4]

While the earliest house, Sunnyside Street, had no traditional features at all, a classical flavour developed markedly from one scheme to the next in those that followed: the Serliana which is merely a shingle style porch in the second house, Lake Street, becomes the entire facade in the last, the Doric House. The use of the Doric architrave to bind the two parts of this house together – the grandiose classical billboard in the front being tied back to the cheap Californian bungalow in the rear – suggests a marked advance in Smith's understanding of the potential application of the classical canon. Despite the Venturian "decorated shed" approach to the house as a whole, Smith treated the Doric architrave in a rather sophisticated fashion. He omitted the triglyphs in the frieze, but indicated where they would have been by retaining the regularly-spaced guttae and regulae below the taenia. He may have been inspired by Maybeck's use of this device on a window sill in the Oscar Maurer studio house in Berkeley, or by an earlier European source with which he was familiar: the early sixteenth-century Villa delle Torre at Fumane near Verona.[5]

At the end of this year, Smith returned to Europe with the funds from the John K. Branner travelling fellowship he had been awarded by Berkeley on his

Jefferson Street House. from SW

above: Jefferson Street House, perspective drawing

below left: Kilian Ignaz Dientzenhofer, S. Florio, Kladno

below right: Ludwig Mies van der Rohe, Tugendhat House, Brno

graduation. He had been forced to postpone it from the previous summer because Marika was then pregnant with their first child, Alan, who was born in October 1975. This trip, primarily to Central Europe, was planned beforehand in minute detail, enabling him to see as much as possible in the shortest time. This highly prepared approach to travel, marking up maps and assembling home-made guidebooks of all the buildings he wished to see in advance, benefited Smith on numerous occasions and is indicative of his voracious appetite for architectural inspiration. The purpose of this trip was twofold: first to see Kilian Ignaz Dientzenhofer's work, exuberant masterpieces of Bohemian Baroque architecture, and at the same time to look at examples of early modernism, in particular buildings by Le Corbusier, André Lurçat, Walter Gropius and Mies van der Rohe.[6] The seeming contradiction in pursuing these divergent interests was already apparent to Smith. Yet what primarily appealed to him about early modernist buildings were their expressionistic qualities and the invigorating freshness of Bohemiam cubism; aspects which were rapidly lost as the movement spread and became formulaic. Smith's appreciation of the dialectic between classicism and modernism is evident from the visual dichotomy in the Doric house and this conflict between innovation and tradition was soon to become central to his work.

House at Tagachang Beach, Guam

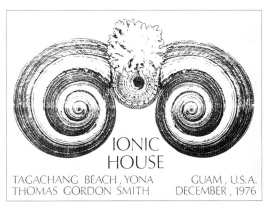

Ionic House, Tagachang Beach, Guam
Brochure cover with Thun shell capital

On Smith's return to the States, the firm for which he worked in the Bay Area sent him to the island of Guam, in the Pacific Ocean. A typhoon had recently hit the island causing some destruction and resulting in Congress allocating funds for emergency relief. The Navy decided to spend some of this money on installing central air conditioning in the homes occupied by their personnel. Smith therefore spent six months measuring all the windows in hundreds of identical Navy-built houses. He alleviated the boredom of this soul-destroying task by developing his own hypothetical projects, again thinking in terms of a house for his family though he never seriously intended to remain on the island. This time he chose a breath-taking site on Tagachang Beach with spectacular views out over the Pacific Ocean.

While one might have imagined that his previous house projects for Bay Area sites had a strong regional flavour because he had grown up surrounded by Californian bungalows and Craftsman houses, Smith

Ionic House, Tagachang Beach, Guam
perspective of site

exhibited in Guam an impressive facility for immersing himself in the local vernacular. The low-slung form, hipped corrugated roof and pigment stained concrete block walls resemble the "boonie" huts which were a common sight on the island. He also demonstrated, for the first time in his work, the flexibility of the classical canon in accommodating variations derived from the indigenous culture. For instance, the Ionic capitals in the living room were to be executed in terracotta following the form of the native Thun shell, and the columns of the deep portico wrapped around the house were to be betel-nut palm trunks, the slight swelling of which he observed bore a resemblance to the entasis of classical columns. Most striking of all, however, was the introduction of Baroque elements in the plan of the house, with an oval living room and a semi-outdoor elliptical terrace articulating a shift in axis. Here, Smith was clearly trying to apply the lessons he had learnt from his detailed study of Dientzenhofer's dynamic handling of space to a contemporary building.

To combat the sense of isolation Smith felt in Guam he prepared a small brochure on this project, sending fifty copies to people he thought might be interested, in particular to those he viewed as his intellectual mentors. These included Christian Norberg-Schulz, the architect and professor at the University of Oslo. While Smith had not yet met him, it had been Norberg-Schulz's

1968 book on Dientzenhofer and Bohemian Baroque architecture which had inspired Smith to take his recent influential trip to Bohemia.[7] Norberg-Schulz responded to the brochure with enthusiasm, writing that he found Smith's approach "fascinating," that he admired his "sensitive interpretation of Baroque themes" and expressing the desire to follow the progress of Smith's work and write about it.[8]

Another fruitful friendship which resulted from sending out a brochure was Charles Jencks, who was then teaching at the University of California at Los Angeles. Jencks, born in America but trained as an architectural historian in Britain under Reyner Banham, was the earliest and most influential historian of Post-modernism. He developed a diagram, reminiscent of those devised by palaeontologists to show evolutionary sequences, which he used to illustrate the traditions within twentieth-century architecture.[9] He constantly updated this evolutionary tree, as he called it, and he included "Tom Smith" in one of the first he drew up to delineate the main strands within Post-modernism. While Smith was undoubtedly delighted to be listed in such a setting by Jencks, he tactfully asked "if you republish the Genealogy of Post-modern Architecture would you please change the abbreviation of my name to Thos. G. Smith."[10]

Richard Long Houses

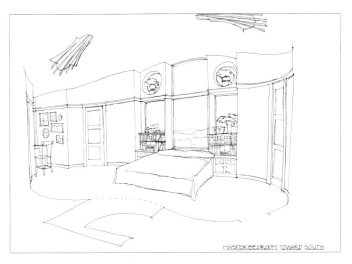

Richard Long House I, Carson City, Nevada, interior view

On his return, Smith continued to eke out a living with various firms, including some work with the distinguished urbanist Dan Solomon, for whom he drew images of appropriate streetscapes for the city of San Francisco. He supplemented this work with a commission from Dr Richard Long, his first real client. Long, an old friend of Smith's father-in-law, had recently moved to Carson City, Nevada, and was considering building a house on a majestic desert site surrounded on all sides by distant mountains. Smith's response to this commission was a series of three designs developed over a two year period. While many of Smith's ideas delighted the client, so that he noted on one sketch that "after a great deal of thought I think your bedroom is basically .... Wow!!!,"[11] none of the completed schemes ultimately satisfied him, with the result that, even after the third design, he commented: "Still nothing to build." The process had, however, allowed Smith to develop his application of Baroque planning techniques in a domestic setting to a considerable level of sophistication. In the first design the house is broken down into a series of pavilions organised around an oval terrace. Externally, a large thermal window is folded around a corner; it lights the only second-storey space, an "aero-plane room" which provides a panoramic view of the desert. The exterior is also enlivened by elaborate Michelangelesque door

cases, picked out in bright colours in a foretaste of the powerful polychromy that would become almost a hallmark of Smith's work over the next decade. Inside, he experimented with great spatial complexity in individual rooms, so that an entry sequence consists of a series of elliptical spaces linked by a sinusoidally curving hall, and a kidney-shaped main bedroom had a shower laid out in the form of the spiral of an Ionic volute. As yet, however, none of these spaces interacted to produce a legible whole, each elaborate volume being cushioned by wasted poché, like the holes in Swiss cheese.

Extensive discussions with Charles Jencks, who came to stay with Smith early in 1978, and their subsequent correspondence help to explain ideas which lay behind the design of the Long House. Smith described the plan to him in terms of an analogy with the digestive system as though "the forms [are] contracting and conducting visitors to the next chamber" rather like the gut propelling a bolus of food along its length, but Smith also admitted that the metaphor was a refinement which was "made after the plan had been developed for formal and spatial reasons" and that "the experience of space, vistas and light is more important."[12] In fact, to emphasize that it was a visual effect that Smith was looking for primarily, he explained what he was trying to achieve in cinematic terms: "From mid-point in the foyer the vista through the serpentine hall reveals half-

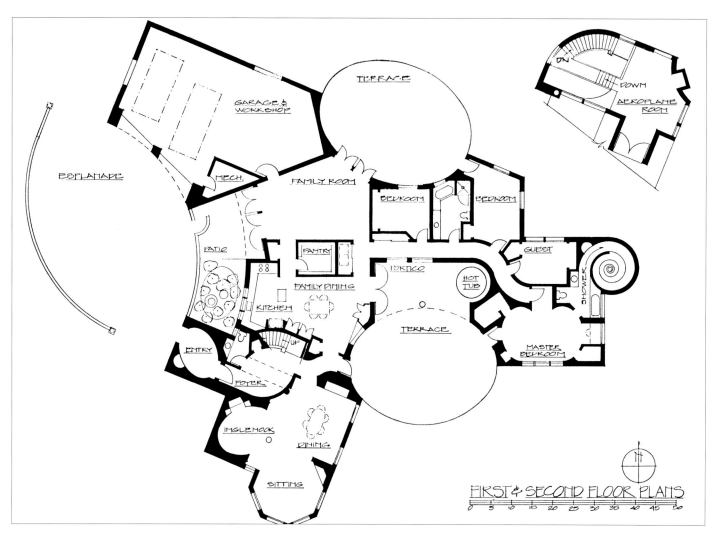

FIRST & SECOND FLOOR PLANS

above: Richard Long House II, Carson City, Nevada, first and second floor plans

opposite above left: Richard Long House II, perspective

opposite above right: Richard Long House II, interior view

opposite below: Richard Long House I, perspective

building, half-landscape. I hope that one's vision while walking through the hall will be like a 'pan' in film. At one point the door frame will be revealed, then pan out to only landscape." Smith described how in the bedroom, similarly, the formal aspects of the design preceded the iconographic: "I began the bedroom plan as a simplified version of Dientzenhofer's St Xavier. The phallic allusion became apparent later and [was] in this case appropriate to exploit." Smith went on to explain his objection to a recent project where the entire plan took the form of a phallus: "My objection to

Tigerman's Daisy house is that it expresses a single idea – it seems obsessive [while] I'm striving for a richness of meaning." Of course, the "obsessive" phallomorphism of the Daisy House (1975-77) may be seen as justified since Stanley Tigerman had designed it for the owner of a strip joint.[13]

The second design for the Long House is the most highly developed of the three, going so far as to note in detail the placement of furniture. Here the continuously curving sinusoidal roof of the first scheme was replaced by a series of rational pitched roofs with broad Tuscan overhangs, defining each separate block of the

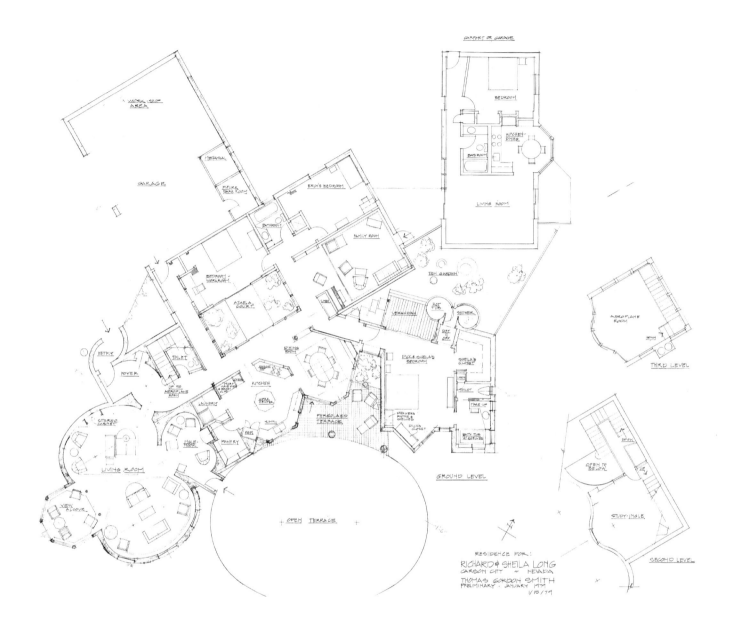

above and opposite: Richard Long House II, Carson City, Nevada, plans

house. The rusticated exterior walls are articulated by stripped down pilasters, in the manner of Robert Stern [and Philip Johnson?], disposed according to the proportions recommended by Vitruvius for a Tuscan temple, and complemented by appropriately corniced and pedimented windows. Inside, the most complex spatial arrangement is reserved for the quatrefoil living room, a clear forerunner of the one Smith created later for his own Richmond Hill House. The main volume of the room is defined by two parallel ellipses which flank an axis running from a kidney-shaped inglenook to an octagonal window bay. This attempt to create a number of volumetrically complex interdependent spaces is clearly inspired by Guarini and Dientzen-hofer. On one of the side walls of the living room, a cabinet for the display of Native American artifacts is framed by an elaborate mural in the Third Style of ancient Roman wall painting,

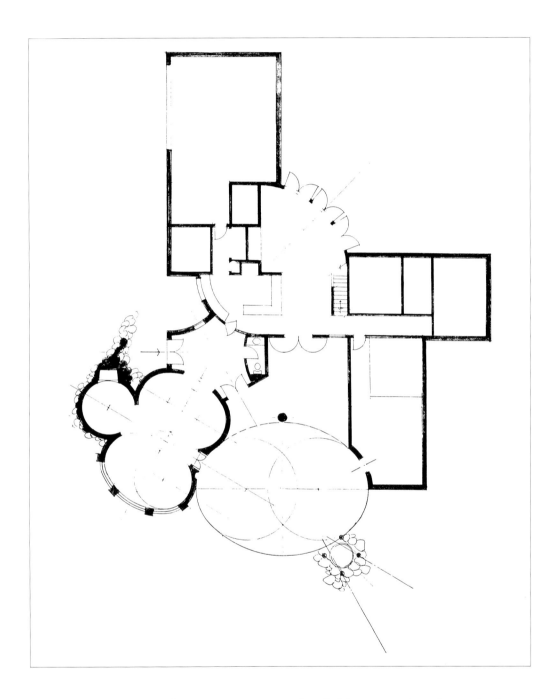

following examples from the House of Livia in Rome. The fictive columns of the mural, which cast faux shadows on the wall, have real counterparts framing the entrance to the window bay.

Though the third scheme for Dr Long was not developed to as advanced a stage as the second, here Smith succeeded in completely resolving the spatial complexities with which he had been struggling. An authentically Baroque spatial sequence was achieved in the fluid progression through the main ceremonial spaces of the house: foyer, living room, inglenook and terrace. The rusticity of the Tuscan living room pavilion was further enhanced by the use of rough boulders for the chimney, the exterior walls of the inglenook and the bases of the concrete block piers, in a manner recalling the work of Californian Arts and Crafts architects, such as Maybeck or Greene and Greene.

above: Richard Long House III, Carson City, Nevada, perspective view of bay window

below: Richard Long House III, Carson City, Nevada, perspective

The Quonset Hut Houses:
Paulownia, Shell and Matthews Street

above left: Paulownia House, colour perspective

above right: Paulownia House, view from bedroom

The tension which is apparent between the formal articulation of the classical canon and the vernacular constructional techniques in the Long series, became even more evident in the houses Smith continued to design for his family over the same two year period, from 1976 to 1978. While in Guam, Smith had been struck by the Baroque spatial qualities of an extremely humble form of building: the Quonset hut. These temporary structures were originally built for military storage purposes, with examples scattered all over the island, but by the 1970s the form was primarily being manufactured for agricultural functions. It occurred to Smith that this might be the solution to his quest to create a noble space for his own home on a minimal budget. His first design based on the hut was called, appropriately enough, the Quonset house.

Smith's second quonset-based design was for a site in Oakland and was called the Paulownia House. While in Guam, Smith's voracious appetite for architectural inspiration had taken him on a three week trip to Japan, and like his masters Maybeck and Wright he returned tremendously impressed by the traditions of Japanese timber construction. The Paulownia flower is a motif of Japanese heraldry and was used by Smith as a decorative emblem throughout the house. In addition, the main bedroom had a raised tatami mat sleeping platform opening on to a wooden deck, beyond which extended a traditional raked Japanese garden. Here, the only plantings were Paulownia saplings and a Wisteria trailing over the trellis roof of the deck. A series of irregular paving stones led to a tiny Japanese bathhouse with a curved roof faintly echoing in miniature the corrugated roof of the quonset hut which enclosed the main spaces of the house.

For the exterior of this house Smith employed a complete polychromatic palette for the first time, with the entire ground floor executed in bands of red and grey, the upper floor solid yellow, and all the woodwork blue. The inspiration for this dramatic experiment was an exhibition of eighteenth- and nineteenth-century student work from the Ecole des Beaux-Arts in Paris organised by Arthur Drexler at the Museum of Modern Art in New York. The exhibition which opened in October 1975, included numerous archaeological *envois* executed in the early nineteenth century by French students on trips to Greece and Sicily. One notable example was Henri Labrouste's reconstruction of the Temple of Hercules at Cora (1831), which Drexler subsequently used for the cover illustration of his book on this subject.[14] In much the same way as these colourful drawings shocked the architectural establishment when they were first

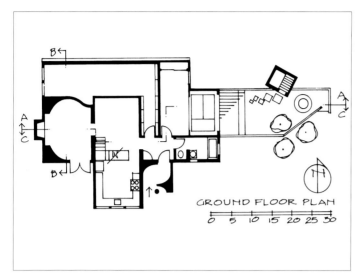

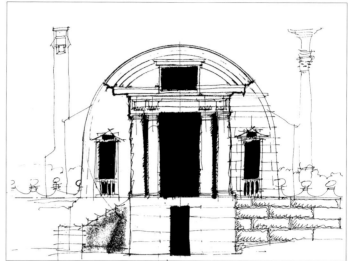

above left: Paulownia House, plan

above right: Shell House, elevation sketch

executed, this exhibition demolished the current preconception of ancient Greek architecture as cold and rational, precisely those qualities which had appealed to early modernists, reconfirming instead that it was resplendent with colour. The contemporary interest shown in polychromy by American architects is amply demonstrated by Charles Moore's Piazza d'Italia in New Orleans, the design of which was developed around the same time as the exhibition even though construction of this seminal post-modernist work was not completed until 1978.

The quonset hut also formed the basis of the second of his house projects during these years, the Shell house which Smith cheekily proposed for a site adjacent to Bernard Maybeck's Wallen W. Maybeck House of 1937. Maybeck built this innovative house high up on the ridge of the Berkeley Hills for his son when he himself was in his mid-seventies and it now belonged to friends of Smith. In order to ensure the house would be fireproof and economical to build, Maybeck had employed a range of industrial materials and building products in its construction: the roof was corrugated steel, the walls a sandwich of concrete and insulating cement mixed with rice hulls poured in modular steel forms, the windows industrial steel sash and the unique heating system even used a radiator from a Model T

Ford.[15] Yet, despite this choice of materials, Maybeck imbued the house with a sense of human scale and dignity through the adoption of highly traditional forms, such as pronounced Tudor gables and a large oriel window. Smith had been fascinated by this house since he was a teenager and it was precisely this unlikely combination of industrial materials and traditional forms which inspired Smith to attempt the same in the Shell house. The quonset hut here became the governing factor in the overall form of the house, unlike its role in the Paulownia house where its presence was downplayed. At the front, the curve of the corrugated roof was emphasised by a powerful Michelangelesque pediment supported by four Doric columns and an abbreviated entablature. The tympanum was pierced by a single window and the portico was flanked by two more surrounded by aedicules. The chimney to one side of the hut follows those of the Maybeck house in the bare functionality of its concrete form. When seen from the front, this appears to be balanced by a single freestanding Corinthian column, though this actually stands in the garden behind the house. This playful contrast, between the utilitarian modernism of the chimney and the decorative classicism of the garden ornament, encapsulates the central dichotomy of Smith's work at this period,

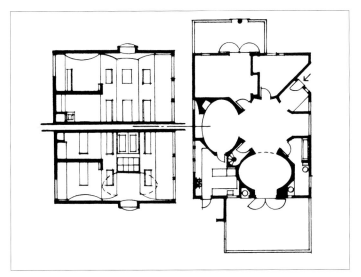
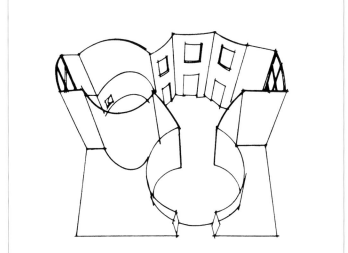

Quonset House, plan and section

generating a tension of which he was quite conscious and indeed exploited to considerable effect.

A clue to the direction in which this tension might be resolved was given in the most fully developed of Smith's projects for a house for his family, the Matthews Street House. He began the design with highly practical considerations in mind – for reasons of economy it was based again on a quonset hut and the classical detailing would be provided by three Doric columns which Smith, since the age of fifteen, had known were for sale, chained to the outside of a Berkeley antique shop. These budgetary constraints were soon abandoned however, with the final design calling for a conventional wood frame construction and four rather than three columns for the portico. The colourful palette of the Paulownia house now became a fully resolved Beaux-Arts restitution of ancient Greek polychromy with each element picked out in vibrant colours following Bernard Loviot's *envoi* of the Parthenon which had been exhibited at MOMA.[16]

A visible separation between the formal double height living hall and the main body of the house was achieved through the external division into two distinct blocks painted in different colours, peach and Chinese green, in this case a rather more subtle polychromy based on Maybeck's work. Within, a final flicker of

oriental influence remained with an internal oriel window placed high above the staircase in a fashion consciously modelled on a nineteenth-century Japanese tea merchants' town house which Smith had seen reconstructed at Meiji-mura. Many of the classical details, including the portico and the doorway marking the separation of the formal and informal areas, were inspired by those of Michelangelo's Laurentian library. In front of the circular terrace which extended forward from the portico stood a single Corinthian column. This signified, in Smith's words, "the potential for the regeneration of classical architecture typical of the Corinthian."[17]

In examining all these projects for the Smith family house, one has a sense of the same elements being endlessly transposed and rearranged, rather as though one is looking through a constantly revolving kaleidoscope. And yet a clear progression can be divined. The apparent internal tension which was initially supplied through the opposition of classical detail and modern form or materials, was now finally being expressed through mannered departures from the classical canon. In the Matthews Street house, the columns of the two storey portico are not evenly arranged on all three sides, or even just across the front, but irregularly disposed to one side and combined with

Thomas Gordon Smith

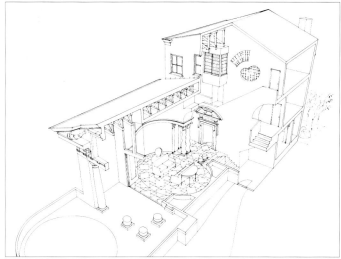

opposite: Matthews Street House, Berkeley, perspective with column

above left: Matthews Street House, Berkeley, perspective showing neighbours

above right: Matthews Street House, Berkeley, cutaway drawing of model

an anta extension of the wall. A rational explanation might be provided in the need to shield the portico from the neighbouring house to the north, and to give it a Southwestern aspect to catch the sun. Yet, the result runs so contrary to the classical canon that it was, without any doubt, the quirky and unorthodox visual effect which was paramount.

Smith used the development of the Matthews Street house to illustrate his design process in an article he wrote for an issue of the *Journal of Architectural Education* for an issue which Richard B. Oliver guest edited. Oliver, the curator of Architecture and Design at the Cooper-Hewitt museum in New York, had included seven of Smith's drawings and a model in the *Ornament* exhibition he organised at the Cooper Hewitt at about the same time. Smith began the article by stating succinctly that "Eclecticism is a method of architectural design, not a style. I am eclectic in my approach to design. I draw my sources from tradition, then re-draw them to contribute new forms to tradition."[18] Lest anyone should mistake him for "an applied archaeologist," in the words of Claude Stoller's quip of half a dozen years earlier, he continued: "I use elements of historical design in my work. I maintain that the results are different from the antiquarian's academic exercise for historical revival. I reject a doctrinaire approach to sources." The article was profusely illustrated with design development sketches and photographs of models of the Matthews Street House. Smith explained how he used sketching to develop the design, beginning first in abstraction without attention

to context, and gradually adding ideas and paying attention to the contingencies of the actual site. Then he would elaborate the details, for instance he traced the outline of a doorframe by Michelangelo from a slide of the original, enlarged it and applied the motif to the pediment. Scaled elevation drawings followed next, resulting in geometrical impossibilities being resolved and some elements discarded. Then a simple foam core model is built using copies of plans and elevations. This is photographed from eye-level vantage points so that the negatives can be projected in order to trace perspective drawings; similarly, the model is cut open and photographed to prepare an aerial cutaway drawing. This type of drawing conveys spatial relationships as well as an axonometric does, but without its disconcertingly technical effect.

Smith raised his concerns about the validity of literal classicism in contemporary architecture in his discussions with Charles Jencks, who came with his wife Maggie to stay with the Smith family again in early 1979. As Smith wrote to Jencks immediately afterwards: "Our meetings were very thought provoking. I am especially intrigued by your thoughts about the fine line between good kitch (*sic*) and bad kitch, OK pastiche and pastiche. Also the danger of period revivalism. I see two ways to interpret the eclecticism of Maybeck and Lutyens. One, as a model, an approach to be emulated to produce new forms which expand and enrich the traditions; two, the approach of seeing it was a period [style] (which I have trouble doing so objectively) and reviving its forms literally."[19]

Tuscan and Laurentian Houses

opposite: Tuscan and Laurentian Houses, Livermore, view of internal courtyard

above: Laurentian House, view of entrance

Despite the fruitless outcome of their earlier introduction of Smith to Richard Long, Marika's parents attempted to help again, this time by commissioning two houses from him as a speculative venture. For inspiration for these Tuscan and Laurentian houses, as Smith was to call them, he turned to classical literature.

Pliny the Younger's epistolary descriptions of two of his villas have been a source of inspiration to architects since the Renaissance.[20] While extremely evocative of the charms of villa life, Pliny was remarkably vague on the question of architectural details. Nevertheless, it is perhaps Pliny's vagueness which explains his appeal to so many architects who have reconstructed the villas as a vehicle for their own ideas. Rarely have these reconstructions been built, almost all remaining as drawings or even models. Like many before him, Smith did not attempt an authentic archaeological reconstruction of these villas, but instead allowed the general character and sense of place conveyed by Pliny to influence him in the designs for these two speculative houses.

While the houses are of necessity set back from the street in a conventional suburban fashion, the space between them is cleverly defined by setting the Laurentian house a short distance behind its own garage to create a small, almost urban space, which Smith referred to in the plans as a piazzetta. This area, which is paved in an elliptical fashion, corresponds to Pliny's description of a sheltered courtyard in the shape of the letter O within his villa at Laurentinum. This piazzetta allows the main rooms of the Tuscan house to be primarily oriented to the South without being shaded. This arrangement is additionally helped by the adoption of what is known in the South as "Charleston manners" whereby the Laurentian house has no North facing windows to overlook its neighbour a mere ten feet away.

At first glance these houses might appear to be conventional Californian bungalows which had merely been brightly painted and to which a scattering of architectural salvage had been applied; closer examination, however, reveals a sensitive choice of colour and meaningful use of the orders. The hierarchical relationship between the Laurentian garage and house is marked by the progression from a rustic Tuscan treatment of the garage with its rough-hewn trunk column and deep overhanging eaves to the sophisticated use of Doric columns in full polychromy to frame the door of the main house like a triumphal arch. The three columns used for this applied framing device were those initially destined for the Matthews Street house, and here again Smith uses them as an unorthodox group of three specifically to signal his

above: Tuscan and Laurentian Houses, Livermore, view from street

opposite: Tuscan House, Living room

departure from the canon. In the Tuscan house all the columns used – at the entrance to the garage, on the two-storied screen of superimposed columns and within the house – are variants on the Tuscan. Hierarchy is present, however, in that internally they are used with a simple entablature, but externally without one.

The Tuscan house is markedly more ambitious in its internal disposition than its neighbour. Behind the arcuated columnar screen facing the piazzetta there is a small courtyard on to which all the major ground floor rooms open, rather like the impluvium of an ancient villa. On axis with the entrance screen is a double height cruciform living room modelled after the salone of Palladio's Villa Foscari. Unlike the original, the geometry of the vault is planar for reasons of economy. In the Vitruvian House of a dozen years later Smith could afford to create proper barrel vaults and achieve more closely the same effect as Palladio. Light enters on three sides, though it is most dramatically handled on the West where daylight is brought through a concealed opening to flood a niche. This Baroque conceit was familiar to Smith from examples such as Bernini's Cornaro Chapel in Santa Maria della Vittoria in Rome

as well as instance in the work of Vittone and Guarini. In the Laurentian house the plan is simpler and compact, the only feature especially worthy of note being a short elliptical passage leading from the hall to the living room designed to ensure that one enters the room on axis with the hearth. This technique of using a diagonal corridor to reorient the visitor had been used by Robert Venturi in his Vanna Venturi house, and again a few years later by Robert Stern in his Lang residence, Connecticut of 1973-4.[21] Smith was, however, primarily familiar with the device from its use by Sir Edwin Lutyens at Folly Farm, Sulhampstead, Berkshire, England.

By the time the construction of these houses was complete, the Californian real estate market was experiencing one of its periodic downturns. Thus, in spite of Smith's carefully considered designs and the extensive publication of these houses in magazines such as *House and Garden* and *House Beautiful*,[22] they lingered unsold for numerous months, and in desperation the contractor finally painted the Laurentian house white in the hope of securing a speedier sale.

CHAPTER III

Rome and the Venice Biennale

"Smith stands alone in America …
in the haunting aura with which he can endow his images"
Vincent Scully

opposite: Strada Novissima façade, view at an angle

above: St Vianney, Rome, interior perspective across altar

As his interest in canonic classicism grew Smith came to realise that what he needed more than anything else was a prolonged period of study in Rome. He had accordingly submitted applications for a fellowship to the American Academy in Rome. In 1978, after two unlucky submissions, he was successful and was awarded the coveted Rome Prize. The jury that year consisted of, amongst others, Charles Moore, Stanley Tigerman and Romaldo Giurgola. Smith had met Moore, a former chairman of the school of architecture at Berkeley, when he was the guest speaker at Smith's own graduation ceremony there in 1975. And while Smith confesses to not having even heard of Moore when he began his architectural degree, his designs immediately after graduation show a clear knowledge of Moore's residential work. Though the senior architect was never to go as far as advocating a literal revival of the classical tradition, Moore showed an appreciation of the human need for ornament and the value of historical precedent. In fact, one common interest which brought

above: St Vianney, Rome, detail of angel with bell

below: St Vianney, Rome, plan

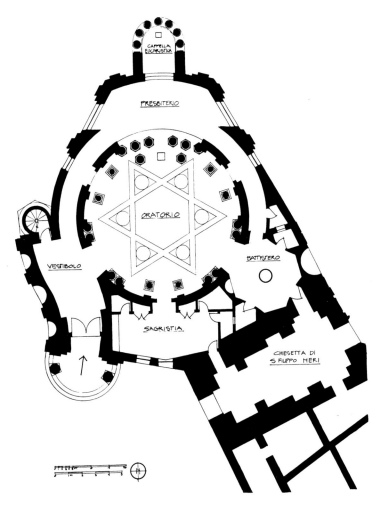

Smith and Moore together at this time, was their shared enthusiasm for using architectural salvage in contemporary buildings. Moore came to San Francisco from Los Angeles in 1979 to speak in a public lecture series organised by Smith. While visiting, he admired an oval dormer window from a recently-demolished residence for the elderly, St. Anne's Home, San Francisco, which Smith was intending to use over the front door of his Tuscan house. Subsequently, Smith sent Moore a drawing of one of the dormers, and details of their price ($100) and the address of the salvage firm which was selling them.[1] Moore subsequently incorporated one of these window frames in the interior of his own apartment in the Moore Rogger Hofflander Condominium, Los Angeles, which he was then just completing.[2] Apparently it was Moore who, on opening Smith's portfolio, immediately insisted to the rest of the jury that this was the person to whom they should award the prize that year.

The impact on Smith of this year in Rome was as much a result of his contact with the distinguished scholars at the American Academy, as his exposure to the extraordinary buildings of the eternal city. Smith had not by then and was in fact never to have the opportunity of working closely with a great architect in the traditional relationship of apprentice to master. At the academy, on the other hand, he was to develop a close working relationship with a number of historians. Joseph Connors, a professor at Columbia University, had trained as an architectural historian under Richard Krautheimer, James Ackerman and Henry Millon at Harvard. He was working on one of the greatest misunderstood geniuses of Roman Baroque architecture, Francesco Borromini, publishing his seminal study of Borromini's Roman Oratory in the following year, 1980.[3] Both Connors and Smith shared an interest in the rigour of Borromini's architecture and his profound understanding of the classical canon, qualities which had not previously been appreciated by critics. Smith's second major influence was an art historian, John Beldon Scott, who was working on the iconography of the Pietro da Cortona's ceilings at the Palazzo Barberini.[4] Before Smith collaborated with Scott none of his projects had a developed programme

of iconography, though his interest in the potential of architectural ornament to carry meaning is apparent from examples in his designs such as the Paulownia flower or the lone Corinthian column as a symbol of rebirth. Afterwards, as we shall see, Smith's work would consistently feature elaborate iconographic programmes executed either in fresco or sculpture.

The third figure in Rome to have a particular impact on Smith during his residence at the Academy was the Revd George Rutler, an Episcopalian priest who was studying at the Angelicum Papal Institute in preparation for his conversion to the Roman Church. He helped develop a programme for the major design project Smith undertook during his year in Rome: an oratory dedicated to St Jean-Baptiste Marie Vianney.

Vianney (1786-1859) was the parish priest of the Southern French town of Ars for nearly forty-two years from 1815. He was famous for his dedication to his duty as a Confessor, hearing confessions for up to sixteen hours a day. Pius XI canonised him in 1925 as patron of the clergy, and he was popularly known as the Curé d'Ars. The site chosen by Smith for his proposed oratory was an empty triangular lot at the Northern end of the Via Giulia, next to a disused eighteenth-century church dedicated to S. Filippo Neri. The public entrance to the oratory is through a semi-circular portico on a piazzetta at the end of Via Monserrato. The central circular space of the oratory has a Star of David inlaid in its floor, representing the foundation of the church in Hebrew theology and reminiscent of Borromini's use of a similar motif in Sant'Ivo. Each of the six triangles of the star is inset with a circular medallion in mosaic representing one of the six virtues of the Virgin at the time of the Annunciation, the moment when the Law was fulfilled and the Virgin became the first tabernacle of Christ, thus supplanting the synagogue.

The three main liturgical functions of the oratory – preaching, celebrating the Eucharist and hearing confessions – are physically separated so that their related spaces are organised along three different axes within the church: the Eucharistic, Oratorical and Penitential. The Eucharistic axis begins in the sacristy, continues through the altar and presbytery, ending in

the chapel of the Eucharist, occupying the apex of the triangular site. The Penitential axis begins in the ambulatory on one side of the central space, and terminates on the other in the octagonal baptistery with its flanking confessionals. Between these two, lies the oratorical axis, leading from the vestibule to the pulpit opposite. These three axes are reinforced spatially by the articulation of the walls and the hemispherical dome. Freestanding and partially engaged columns and pilasters support a Doric entablature from which a brick vault rises. The altar is flanked on either side by clusters of four columns, set apart by their unusual hexagonal bases and with Eucharistic symbols in the metopes of the frieze above. The iconographic programme continues in the stained glass windows of the presbytery beyond, where angels are depicted with the instruments of Christ's passion.

Within the solid structure of the brick vault, a much lighter hemispherical baldacchino floats, appearing to billow upwards like a sail. This inner layer consists of interlocking segments of an ogival vault springing without an entablature from three pairs of marble Solomonic columns. The columns are supported by pulvinated bases and are finished with the texture of tree bark which symbolizes the human quality required for the ministry. One of these pairs flank the pulpit, above which floats a statue of St Jean Vianney. Still higher, framed by the vault, is a stained glass window featuring the Bible with seven seals and the Lamb of God. These symbols represent the Divine Wisdom towards which both the saint and preacher aspire. The design of the exterior of the oratory was never completely resolved, though Smith developed some schematic sketches showing a tower crowned by the bell which St Jean hung on his church at Ars to mark the completion of its restoration.

While this project was only an academic exercise, its completion was given a huge impetus when Christian Norberg-Schulz informed Smith at a Christmas party that he had been selected as one of the main participants in the Venice Biennale for the next year. The result was months of intense activity for Smith as he designed and constructed his exhibition, and redrew a number of his previous projects for presentation.

The Strada Novissima

opposite: St Vianney, Rome, interior perspective towards altar

above: Strada Novissima façade, close-up view

The organisation of the international architectural exhibition for the 1980 Venice Biennale was given to Paolo Portoghesi, whom Smith had first met by chance eight years previously.[5] Of a total of seventy-five architects who would be exhibiting, only twenty had been selected to design facades which would be constructed to create an internal street in the former rope factory of the Venice Arsenal. This "Strada Novissima," which had as its theme "The Presence of the Past," proved to be a key event in the establishment of post-modernism as an international movement, with the participation of architects not just from Italy and the United States, but also France, Germany, Spain and Japan.

As might be imagined from the post-modern flavour of the event, most of the contributions were either ironic or abstract in their reference to historical traditions. Smith was almost alone in adopting a literate treatment for his classical facade in the Strada.[6] A pair of giant Doric pilasters, supporting a triglyph frieze, frame a concave niche. The frieze is pierced by a central opening allowing views over the Strada from the gallery above, and is enriched by painted metopes representing Michelangelo and Borromini, the two guiding lights of Smith's vigorous composition. Within the niche there is a secondary order consisting of a pair of freestanding Corinthian Solomonic columns set diagonally to define a shallow elliptical space in front of a doorway. The relationship established between the major and minor order is similar to that used by Michelangelo in his Palazzo dei Conservatori on the Capitoline Hill; Smith was fascinated by the way in which variations on this hierarchical arrangement were used by later architects such as Borromini in his San Carlo alle Quattro Fontane.[7] In Smith's facade the entablature of the minor order follows the curve of the apse flush with the wall plane, only darting forward to hold each column in place. The gently curved wall of the apse is painted with an ambitious iconographic programme.

The Ionic architrave and pediment of the door are both painted in trompe l'oeil, with a single word inscription, ARCHITETTURA, above the opening and a tondo in the tympanum featuring in grisaille the instruments of the architect, including a rule, T-square and dividers. Above the portal three allegorical figures are painted: on one side of the pediment, in light colours *Architettura* and *Disegno* engage in dialogue, while in a much darker hue, their antithesis, *Errore*, turns his back on them looking down to the ground. On either side of the doorway two long rectangular panels contain a total of twelve vignettes of Smith's earlier projects, including the Tuscan and Laurentian houses. The division into two groups, one below

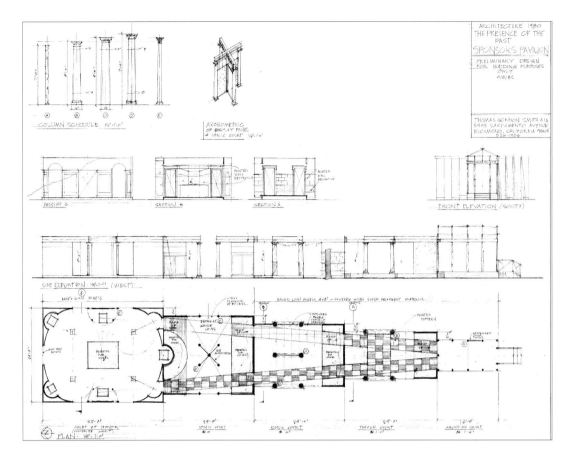

Disegno and the other below *Errore*, indicated which of these earlier projects now still met with Smith's approval. This public act of self-criticism demonstrates how rapidly Smith's architectural convictions had developed during his year in Rome. An exhibition behind the facade displayed full sets of drawings for these projects and for the oratory of St Jean Vianney, the essential architectural elements of which had of course been reconfigured in the facade itself.

Like all the other exhibitors, Smith wrote a statement for the catalogue. Before submitting it for publication, however, he showed it to the Harvard architectural historian James Ackerman who was then staying at the American Academy. As an acknowledged expert on the architecture of Michelangelo, one might have expected Ackerman to have some enthusiasm or at least sympathy for a young practitioner who was clearly so profoundly influenced by the Renaissance master. His written response to Smith's statement, while intended constructively, sums up much of the flawed thinking in the opposition of modernists to a revival of classicism in architecture: "My concern is that for a tradition to function I believe it should be unconsciously shared by most or many members of a society. If you argue for the viability of the classical language you should suggest the way in which a society like ours which has lost contact with it is going to regain contact. You can't simply build classical buildings, like you can't start talking classical Greek and expect people to know what you are saying. ... Why should the classical tradition be given precedence over any major historical model? ... Make me feel that never having wanted to see a classical building made in my lifetime makes me an idiot and forces me to change what I think."[8] It is curious that Ackerman should fall prey to familiar fallacies: unlike language, which needs each individual to learn to speak or read it for it to be "alive", in order for an understanding of an architectural idiom to develop, it simply needs to be seen in the world around us, ordering social and political intercourse through its hierarchy of forms. While few major public buildings in the United States had been built in the classical tradition since John Russell Pope's National Gallery in Washington was completed in 1941, all Americans would be familiar with classical architecture through its use in houses, banks, post offices, railway stations, courthouses, libraries and art galleries in every major city. From the Capitol, the Supreme Court and the White House down to the humblest branch library or post office, the democratic operation of American society was given architectural form through the classical language. Unlike ancient

Greek, this was not a dead language which was lost to obscurity through the passage of two thousand years, but a living tradition which had enjoyed a startling renaissance at the dawn of the twentieth century and was still flourishing four decades later.

In a review of the Biennale, Charles Jencks observed that "Smith is the only architect here to treat the classical tradition as a living discourse."[9] In a fundamental way this was quite literally true. Cinécittà, the film set construction company who were responsible for building the exhibition, told Smith on seeing his design that he would have to modify it as they did not know how to construct the Solomonic columns. Unwilling to compromise his design, he realised that he would have to make the columns himself. Of course, he had no idea how to go about it either, but he began by looking at treatises by Baroque designers to find out. Both Giacomo Barozzi da Vignola in his *La regola delli cinque ordini d'architettura* (1562) and Guarino Guarini in his *Architetura civile* (1737) gave methods for constructing the column mathematically, but Smith found that the clearest method was given by the Jesuit painter and architect, Andrea Pozzo in his *Perspectiva pictorum et architectorum* (1693-1700) which Smith consulted in the Biblioteca Hertziana.[10] This experience of using the same treatises as architects had three centuries earlier,

not merely as a scholarly exercise but as a genuine tool for design and execution, proved to be a formative one for Smith. It gave him an insight into how the classical tradition had been continually developed in the light of contemporary circumstances and then handed on from generation to generation via buildings and treatises.

Despite the small scale of this Biennale project, Smith succeeded in demonstrating to those attending the exhibition the communicative power of the classical tradition both through formal devices, such as the tension between the orthogonal austerity of the Doric frame and the dynamic niche within, and semantic ones, such as the detailed iconographic programme. The Yale architectural historian, Vincent Scully, writing in the catalogue of the Biennale, characterised this quality as follows: "Smith's classical orders begin to resemble those of Maybeck in their Baroque-Primitive power. … Smith stands alone in America, I think, in the haunting aura with which he can endow his images."[11] Almost of greater interest to a student of his work, however, is the way in which Smith managed to convey in his contribution to the Strada Novissima, essentially no more than a giant doorway, all the concerns which were central to his work: colour, spatial dynamism, iconography and, above all, the excitement of the classical canon.

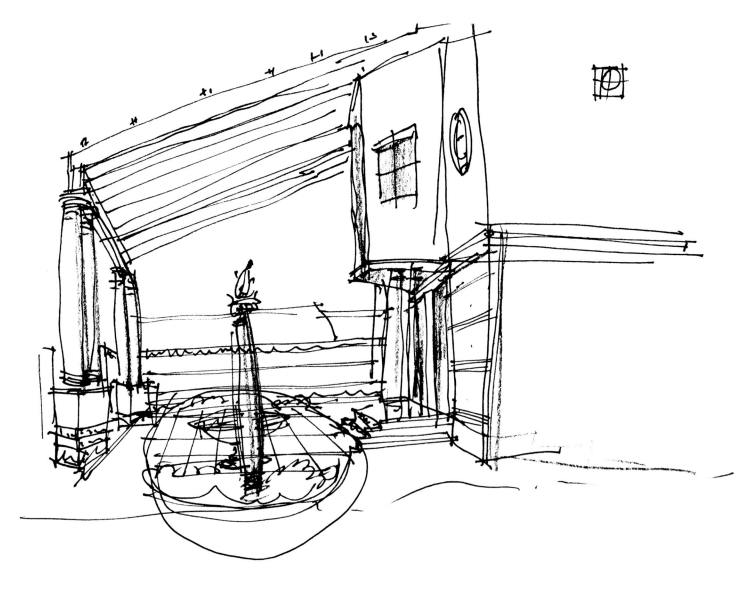

Richmond Hill House, sketch

CHAPTER IV

On Richmond Hill

*"You're internationally recognised – you can't
just work* for *somebody"*
Robert A.M. Stern

At the completion of his year in Rome, Smith was keen to move to New York. He applied for a position with Hardy, Holzman and Pfeiffer, but was unsuccessful. As Robert Stern explained to Smith at the time: "You're internationally recognised - you can't just work <u>for</u> somebody." Deeply despondent, he therefore returned to San Francisco to look for work, though even there he discovered his newly-found fame made it impossible for him to find a job with even a run-of-the-mill firm. As Marika confided in a letter to John Beldon Scott, "After three weeks of hard looking ... he finally got one by going totally incognito because prior interviews with even limited honesty had not seemed to lead to anything."[1]

While Smith worked in the offices of a succession of nobodies, he was able to do a little work of his own on the side. One such project, which came about as a direct result of his involvment in the Biennale, was the design of the Sponsors' pavilion for the recreation of the Strada Novissima at Pier 2 of the Fort Mason Center in San Francisco. A group called "The Friends of the Biennale," of which Smith was a member, raised the necessary funds from developers and architectural firms to bring the original exhibition to the United States in May 1982. The sponsors displayed their promotional material in a pavilion which was 120ft long and, at the broadest point of its tapering plan, 24ft in width. Smith's initial proposal addressed these challenging proportions by breaking the pavilion into a series of five courts, each with its

own order: Composite, Ionic, Doric, Tuscan and Arcadian, with the last being a rustic pergola of slim tree trunks. As finally executed the whole scheme was rather simpler than initially planned, with just three courts, though despite the modifications Smith was still able to explore some of his historical interests by linking the three classical orders, Doric, Ionic and Corinthian, to the First, Second and Third Styles of ancient Roman wall painting.

Another consequence of the Biennale was that Heinrich Klotz, the founding director of the German Architecture Museum, heard of Smith while attending a conference on Alvar Aalto in Finland. Everyone seemed to be complaining about how this completely unknown young American had somehow been included in the prestigious Strada Novissima, while other American architects such as Thomas Beeby, Bill Turnbull and Helmut Jahn had been relegated to small exhibits in the upper galleries of the Arsenale. Intrigued by the depth of jealousy that Smith had provoked, Klotz visited the exhibition and was initially baffled on seeing the four-foot long drawings of the Oratory of St Jean Vianney. How could he have missed this church when he was sure that he knew all the major Baroque monuments in Rome? It was only on closer examination that he realised he was not looking as he first thought at a measured drawing of an existing building, or even a reconstruction of a lost church, but a proposal for a completely new oratory in the heart of historic

Rome. He resolved to meet Smith, and after leaving several telephone messages finally spoke to Marika, announcing that he was "a very important person from Germany" who wished to meet her husband because "I can help him." When Smith drove to meet Klotz, the air of financial need must have been palpable, for Klotz first insisted on filling Smith's car with gasoline before they set off to look at buildings in the Bay Area. The tour proved a success, for Klotz not only offered to buy Smith's entire Biennale exhibit, but also eventually commissioned him to design one of the small garden courts in his new museum in Frankfurt. This transaction was timely, not least because it allowed Smith to realise finally his longstanding desire of buying a lot and building a house for his family.

Richmond Hill House

above: Richmond Hill House, Richmond, section

opposite: Richmond Hill House, Richmond, exterior view in sunlight

The themes which Smith first explored in the Tuscan and Laurentian houses all occur in a more highly developed form in the house which he built for himself on a narrow suburban lot in Richmond, California. Again, for reasons of cost many of the classical elements are supplied by *spolia*, or salvaged materials, from a sanatorium for tuberculosis sufferers in nearby Livermore. This adds an extra layer of complexity to the design process which makes the achievement of this exquisite house seem all the more extraordinary. The entry is framed by two pergolas, supported by pairs of Doric columns and linked by an overarching structure of timber beams which continue the roofline forward. (Note development from earlier scheme where the triglyphs are visible in the extensions of the beams.) In order to gain the necessary building permit this rustic portico was described as a car port to the local planning authority. Its primitive appearance is further enhanced by two ox skulls or bucrania placed above the columns, with red ribbons encircling them in imitation of sacrificial fillets. The front door is flanked by pairs of smaller Tuscan columns which support the projecting dining bay above. The facade is reveted in Texan limestone and reclaimed marble, which forms a suitably neutral backdrop to the intense polychromy of the details: columns in either yellow or Pompeian red, and beams in blue.

Inside, the main living spaces are arranged on the second floor to take advantage of the dramatic view towards the San Francisco bay. The ground floor is therefore tightly planned to accommodate three bedrooms and two bathrooms. As it rises, the main stair is separated from the kitchen/dining room by a single Ionic column supporting a rich Hellenistic en-tablature. Above the kitchen is a galleried bedroom, which is lit by the tall arched window of the dining bay.

None of these ingenious spatial arrangements, however, prepares one for the breathtaking drama of the living room, which forms the climax of the processional route through the house. Here, Smith's studies of Baroque planning and his research on ancient Roman wall painting are fully synthesised. The 20 ft square room is organised along its two diagonal axes. The main axis runs from a niche designed for a virginal, over which a balcony is suspended, to a pair of tall arched windows placed perpendicularly in the opposite corner. These frame views of Mount Tamalpais in the distance. Flanking this axis are two elliptical lozenges marked out in the terrazzo floor with pieces of reclaimed marble in homage to Dientzenhofer's Saint Francis Xavier at Oparany. The mysterious geometric patterns created are reminiscent of the Cosmati work mosaic floors of early mediaeval churches. A secondary axis, perpen-dicular to the first, runs between two book filled niches which occupy the poché created by the curved walls following the outer edges of the two ellipses.

These undulating plaster walls are finished in polished lampblack and marble dust according to ancient fresco recipes. Leaping out from this lustrous black background is an attenuated architectural framework in the third Pompeian style which was painted directly on to the wet plaster by Smith over a four-day period. The thin columns, pilasters and beams are picked out in a dazzling palette of red, yellow, blue and green. Exotic birds perch amongst the garlands of leaves, which hang from the fictive structure, as do red-filleted bucrania, echoing the real skulls outside on the portico. The illusory nature of the architecture is emphasized by the contrast between pictures with painted frames and unframed vignettes emerging directly from the black background. Of the latter those at eye level are either musical trophies, a pair of which flank the virginal's niche, or a brief pictorial history of the gasoline station. Eight different gas stations, one for each decade of the century, are depicted in small vignettes in much the same way that the Romans decorated their houses with pictures of shrines in arcadian settings. These are in reference to the giant oil storage tanks which one can see in the distance towards the bay, the source of Richmond's industrial prosperity. This theme continues in the ceiling with the figure of Petrolia, Smith's invented allegorical figure personifying the petroleum industry, surrounded by representations of the nine ages of man and woman. Smith was initially unsure what theme to use in the

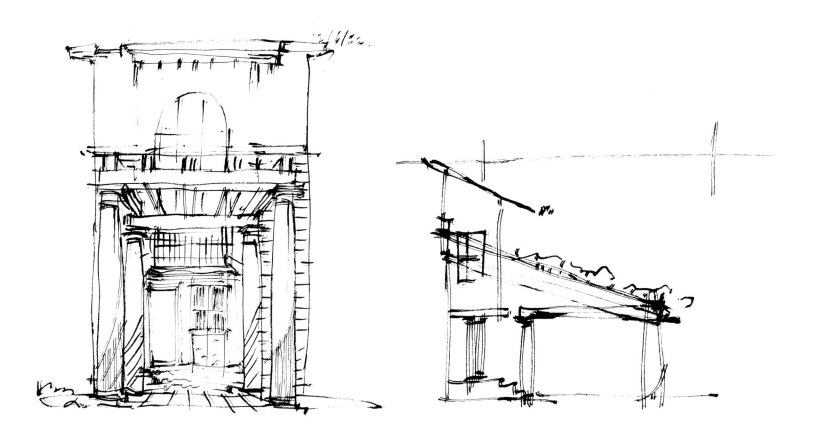

band between the fictive architecture of the walls and the ceiling and so consulted John Beldon Scott asking him for "any ideas for allegories? The cardinal directions bringing goods for oil production from N[orth] S[outh] E[ast] W[est] [or] something to do with place and time would be great."[2] At Scott's suggestion, Smith painted four large scenes from the life of Persephone, featuring Hermes, Demeter and Hades, which represented the passage of the seasons and therefore related to the time needed to produce the "black gold" of Richmond. Finally, there is an inscription on the painted frieze that runs around the entire room:

> On the brow of Richmond Hill
> Which Europe scarce can parallel
> Ev'ry eye such wonders fill
> To view the prospect round
> Where the silver Thames doth glide
> And stately courts are edified.

These words, written by Thomas D'Urfey and set to music in 1692 by Henry Purcell, allude to the original Richmond on the outskirts of London, after which this Californian Richmond was named.

The experience of this room is extraordinarily rich, and assaults the beholder on numerous levels: spatial complexity, intense polychromy, fictive architecture, sophisticated iconography, and even lyric poetry. What Smith has succeeded in creating here, on this conventional suburban lot, adjacent to a declining industrial area, is not an escapist fantasy, but rather an authentic demonstration of how architecture might become, once again, truly meaningful and resonant; how, through visual, literary and mythological allusions, the *genius loci* can be celebrated; and how the act of creating shelter, of building a home, can be elevated to transcend the mundane necessities of humdrum existence to create something spiritually and aesthetically fulfilling.

It is this total approach, encompassing the intellectual as well as the sensual, which again and again would set Smith's architecture apart from the formalism of many of his contemporaries.

above: Richmond Hill House, view of dining room

below left: Richmond Hill House, view of living room towards niche

below right: Richmond Hill House, view of living room towards doorway

opposite: Richmond Hill House, view of living room towards corner window

STATELY COURTS ARE EDIFIED

ON THE BROW OF RICHMO

The Apollo Court, Frankfurt

above: German Architecture Museum, Frankfurt, original scheme

opposite: German Architecture Museum, Frankfurt, second scheme

Heinrich Klotz commissioned eleven architects to design permanent exhibits to fill specially allocated spaces in the German Architecture Museum's new building by Matthias Ungers. The project clearly owed much in its conception to the success of the Strada Novissima, and like the Biennale show it too had a theme, in this case Adam's House or the archetypal shelter. Under pressure from the commissioned architects, however, this theme was soon dropped and Smith, on being given a free rein, chose to develop his space as a shrine to Apollo, ancient god of the sun and the arts.

Smith's design commemorated a particular event described by Ovid in his *Metamorphoses* which had previously inspired Baroque artists and composers such as Bernini and Handel. Daphne, a beautiful but chaste wood nymph, is pursued by the god Apollo, whom Eros has caused to desire her. As the sun god reaches out to grasp her, she cries out for help from her father, the river god Peneus, who in response transforms her into a laurel tree. Smith's first scheme arranged the outdoor space as an apsed court articulated by a primitive Doric order, with a frieze of painted terra-cotta metopes depicting the story of Apollo and Daphne. Though the final design was much simplified, it retained all the basic elements of the earlier scheme: an apse, a central laurel tree representing Daphne, and a freestanding column. The form of the apse was realised in a low hedge of myrtle, while the sacred tree would be a hybrid of the Mediterranean *laurus nobilis* and the Californian bay laurel. Smith himself selected the

actual tree which was sent to Germany. While the first scheme undoubtedly possessed some of the untidy liveliness which characterised the more irrational cults of the ancient Greeks, with its mixture of bizarre orders, rich polychromy and assymmetrically-placed tripod, the second design possessed a simple nobility which was perhaps more appropriate to the contemplative garden court of a museum. The only ornamental elaboration occurs in the column capital which was now Corinthian rather than Ionic. Here, Smith departs from the canon in two ways: laurel leaves replace acanthus in the second register of leaves on the capital, in reference to Daphne's transformation, and bronze flames replace the conventional corner volutes, to indicate its association with the sun-god Apollo.

The tradition of changing the details of the classical orders to express a particular character or association stretches back to antiquity. National identity, for instance, can be expressed through the variation of ornamental details: for example, the use of palm capitals in the Hellenistic period often indicated an association with Pergamum, and a notable later example of this phenomenon is Benjamin Latrobe's use of corn cob capitals in the United States Capitol in Washington. Smith's revival of this tradition highlights one aspect of the enormous potential of the classical canon – precisely because it has a system of commonly accepted rules, conscious deviation from them can be a highly meaningful act.

Lone Mountain, Edgewood Day Center and the Monroe House

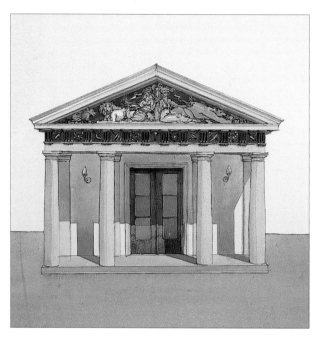

above: Monroe House, Lafayette, elevation of portico

opposite above: Edgewood Day Center, San Francisco, perspective of courtyard

opposite below: Lone Mountain, San Francisco, perspective towards monastery

During this period, Smith ran his first proper office from an attic in downtown San Francisco. It transpired that his own Richmond Hill House would be the only major built work to emerge from this endeavour, but he accepted a number of commissions which had only a relatively remote possibility of being realised. The first such scheme was for a masterplan for Lone Mountain, San Francisco, to accommodate a Jesuit College, a Buddhist monastery, and a mixture of housing and retail. The site, one of the city's many prominent hills, already had a Gothic tower at its highest point. Smith made this carillon the focus of his campus plan, creating a circular piazza in front of it onto which opened a series of internal elliptical courts. To ensure the space was kept free of vehicles and preserved for pedestrian use it would be built one level above grade, creating a large underground parking deck beneath. The piazza is dominated by a central fountain representing the source of the four rivers described in Genesis and taking the form of an obelisk in appropriate homage to Bernini's Four Rivers Fountain in the Piazza Navona, Rome. Water flows from the fountain in the cardinal directions, each stream having a different character. To the South, it flows down the side of the hill which was being left undeveloped in order to preserve the view from the piazza. It runs between existing sets of steps to augment a fountain half way down. To the East and West, the streams have a more natural character: on one side passing through an Oriental garden adjacent to a proposed Buddhist monastery, and on the other becoming a brook for the benefit of the private houses. To the North side, below the chapel, classroom blocks and refectory, an existing dormitory is converted to condominiums and new town houses are added. The urban character of this steep slope is enhanced by shops and restaurants arranged around stepped terraces enlivened by a cascade of fountains. The Mediterranean feel of the planning is further emphasised by the warm coloured render of the new buildings, including the monastery, which is closely modelled on a particular Chinese prototype and is laid out according to the requirements of Feng Shui. The overall development was intended both to help fund the college, and also

above: Lone Mountain, San Francisco, aerial view

opposite above: Monroe House, Lafayette, plan

opposite below: Monroe House, aerial view

to provide a community of residents who would use the college's facilities for cultural events.

A scheme similarly doomed to come to nothing, an extension to the Edgewood Day Treatment Center, was commissioned by one of the trustees of the center, Bea Baldauf, in the hope of persuading her fellow directors. As at Lone Mountain, here Smith had the challenge of a pre-existing building, though in this case the 1920s Renaissance revival orphanage was rather more to his tastes. He broadly replicates the existing building on the other side of a new courtyard, linking the two wings thus created by a raised administrative block. This central pavilion presents an unusual Ionic portico with an arch breaking through the entablature modelled after Palladio's Villa Cerato. On the lower level, a Doric columnar screen running between the flanking wings closes the courtyard to the street and emphasises the hierarchy of the buildings through the use of the orders. Smith here gives ample evidence of his rare skills in creating an addition which both accommodates the complex programme required by a day school for emotionally disturbed children and enhances the existing building. In terms of his architectural development it also represents a substantial

step forward in his appreciation of the classical canon as a hierarchical system which can be used to order and unify a project of remarkable complexity.

The last of the unbuilt projects of Smith's Californian period must have initially appeared to have been the most likely to be realised of the commissions: a suburban house in a warm interior valley in the Bay Area. Smith was recommended to the client, who was highly appreciative of Maybeck's work, by one of his high school friends. Smith tackled the brief by breaking the house down into three pavilions: a two-storey entry block, and two single-storey wings, one for a living room and the other for services. The choice of orders, Ionic for the main block, indicated only by the bed mould and cornice, then Doric and Tuscan for the wings, reflected the hierarchy of uses: public, private and utilitarian. This sequence was even carried through in the proposed roofing materials, with the Ionic block to be roofed in slate, the Doric pavilion in terracotta tile, and the Tuscan wing in wood shingle.

Apart from a Maybeckian concrete chimney, modelled after those of the Wallen Maybeck house, the whole composition was rigorously classical: there were

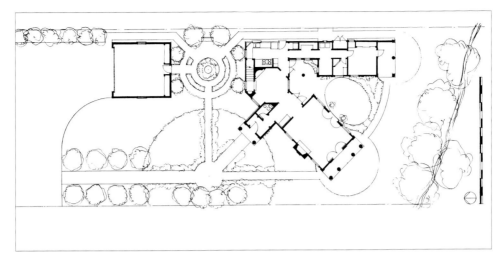

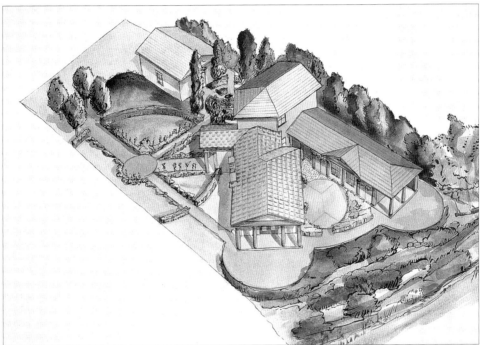

no deliberate solecisms to demonstrate its "modernity." This is not to say, however, it was not without quirks. While most of the metopes of the Doric triglyph frieze were to be filled by low reliefs modelled in terracotta, featuring motifs such as bucrania, a few were to be glazed as windows recalling a similar treatment by Ithiel Town and Alexander Jackson Davis in the side facades of their United States Custom House (1833-42) on Wall Street. Literary evidence for this practice in antiquity is provided by Euripides, one of whose characters expresses their intention of climbing out of a temple through the openings between the triglyphs in the frieze.[3] Even the landscape was purposefully classical, with a formal herb garden placed symmetrically between the main house and the garage.

At its centre, Smith placed a fountain he modelled after one depicted in a vignette in a Pompeian wall painting. Only faint vestiges of Smith's interest in Baroque spatial planning are evident here: externally in an oval terrace between the two wings, and internally through the dramatic "enfilade" created by aligning all the doorways in each wing. Despite advancing to the stage of complete working drawings, the Monroe House was never built, primarily because the contractor's estimate was much higher than the client had originally hoped; the prospects for building the house were not helped, in addition, by the fact that Smith had been offered a permanent position at the University of Illinois at Chicago and had begun preparations to move there from California.

Vitruvian Man and Ionic temple façade

CHAPTER V

Teaching and Scholarship

Reconstruction of the Temple of Apollo, Thermon

"So we'll have Eisenman, the deconstructionist,
and Thomas Gordon Smith, the classicist,
beating up on one another.
What I want is to give the kids a real choice"
Stanley Tigerman

It is rare in the world of contemporary architecture for a practitioner to engage in serious historical scholarship. The discipline of architectural history, once almost solely the preserve of practising architects, is now entirely separated from the creative process. In universities, architectural history is as likely to be taught in a faculty of art history or archaeology as in a school of architecture. Even when it is taught in one, it is treated as though it has almost no relevance to the activities of the design studio. Smith has pursued his scholarly interests at the same time as his creative impulses, allowing the two pursuits to develop in parallel and, in fact, to cross-fertilise one another completely. His earliest interest, the architecture of the Bay area, resulted in Smith helping found the Berkeley Architectural Heritage Association, for which he designed a letterhead. In 1979 he organised a public lecture series entitled "The Challenge of Eclecticism" with sponsorship from the San Francisco Museum of Modern Art and the Northern California Chapter of the American Institute of Architects. The list of lecturers was unusual in featuring both practitioners and historians, and included key figures who had either taught or encouraged him: David Gebhard, Charles Moore, Christian Norberg-Schulz and Michael Graves. In addition, David van Zanten, a young historian who had had been closely involved with the Beaux-Arts exhibition at MOMA, spoke about the system of teaching at the Ecole; and Charles Jencks, the American-born critic and historian who taught at the Architectural Association in London, spoke about "Late Modernism and Post-modernism." Other speakers were Robert A.M. Stern from Columbia University, Robert Judson Clark from Princeton, and John Beach from UCLA. Smith himself spoke fifth in the series, but both his lecture and the series as a whole were greeted with some hostility by the *San Francisco Bay Architects' Review*, despite the fact that it was the official publication of one of the co-sponsors of the series, the Northern California Chapter of the AIA. While acknowledging that the lectures were attracting "standing-room-only crowds (including many non-architects)," Ben Clavan, an editorial board member of the *Review*, pronounced on the front page that they "must be classed with much of the nonsense. It is hardly possible to take someone like Charles Jencks or Thomas Smith seriously."[1] In a review of Smith's own lecture his work was dismissed as "exterior decoration" with "classical motifs ... applied to his structures like the latest trendy dress draped over a French model" and the piece ended mockingly on the same theme: "We are back to the Beaux-Arts through Yves St. Laurent."[2]

Notwithstanding the sniping of such critics, the popular success of this series led Smith into a more ambitious undertaking after his return from Rome: the revitalisation of the San Francisco Architecture Club. This organisation was initially founded in 1901 by nineteen draughtsmen to provide the earliest accredited programme of architectural study in the Bay Area. The curriculum during its earliest decades was supervised by the Beaux-Arts Institute of America, based in New York, and was taught in Ateliers by Patrons such as Arthur Brown, Jr., the architect of San Francisco City Hall, and George Kelham, the architect of the city's Public Library. A few of the students went on to study at the Ecole des Beaux-Arts in Paris, such as the architect of the Golden Gate Bridge, Irving Morrow, but for most the Club's programmes provided the whole of their training. In the post-war period, as university-based schools such as Berkeley became more accessible, the Club's focus shifted towards providing seminars to prepare prospective architects for the State Board's licensing examinations.

The membership gradually dwindled until closure of the club was contemplated in the late 1960s which would have resulted in the dispersal of its library of nineteenth- and early twentieth-century folios. However, a dedicated group of seven members continued to meet on a monthly basis. Members slowly ebbed until 1983 when, with just four left, Smith joined and began his work to revive the club. Tax-exempt charitable status was sought and achieved, the library was rehoused in the Fort Mason Center, and over twenty-five new members were recruited. Smith created an unofficial advisory board which included practitioners of arts other than architecture who were interested in traditional approaches, including the painter David Ligare, the neo-baroque

opera composer Conrad Cummings, and the harpsichordist Jean Nandi who began to teach Smith the instrument in 1984. A new programme of events was introduced with a particular emphasis on providing classes which would not be offered by any other organisation. Their uniqueness partly derived from the subjects of the seminars and workshops, which included "Drawing and Rendering the Classical Orders," "Harmonic Proportions in Classical Architecture" and "The Origins of the Doric Order," but also was a result of having teachers from a range of different disciplines in addition to architecture. These included the archaeologists Margaret Miles and Gretchen Umholtz, and the musicologist, Julie Cumming. Buffet lunches were held to enable members to hear distinguished practitioners, such as Allan Greenberg and Stanley Tigerman, discuss contemporary issues. A major interdisciplinary colloquium on "The Baroque: It's Power Today" was organised by Smith for the club in 1987, even though by the time it occurred he had moved to Chicago. The speakers included the architects Paolo Portoghesi, Charles Moore and Robert Stern, the harpsichordist Davitt Moroney, the composer Lou Harrison, and the art historian John Beldon Scott. The event was accompanied by a performance of two one-act operas performed by Baroque instrument specialists including Handel's *Apollo e Daphne* and a specially commissioned work on the same theme by Conrad Cummings, *Apollo and Daphne* sung by Judith Nelson.[3]

Smith's passion for Baroque architecture in its Bohemian, Piemontese and Roman guises clearly flowered during his Rome fellowship at the American Academy. This interest was undoubtedly motivated by his own personal search for an architectural idiom. What is most striking about his approach, however, is that unlike the conventional architectural historian who has been trained in the tradition of Hegelian historicism and therefore sees the Baroque as occupying a pigeonhole in the museum of styles – after Mannerism and before Neoclassicism, Smith simply sees it as part of the continuous living tradition of classical architecture from which he, as a practitioner, is entitled to draw. In fact, he is convinced that if he fails to assimilate it his work will be the poorer for its exclusion. To assist in this process of understanding and absorption, he forged links with practitioners in other fields of creativity for whom the Baroque provided a meaningful paradigm, doing this in particular as we have seen through the San Francisco Architecture Club. His two other main historical interests, the Greek Revival and Vitruvius, deserve to be considered separately, as the fruits of these researches are quite capable of standing alone in the arena of learning.

In 1984, Smith received a grant from the Graham Foundation in Chicago to write a treatise on classical architecture which, like those by Vitruvius, Palladio and Chambers, would also use his own work to illustrate the points being made. This project was to result in *Classical Architecture: Rule and Invention* (1988) a book which had two main goals: first, to present through a series of case studies of historic buildings Smith's own understanding of how classical architecture developed, its relevance today as a living tradition, and the relationship between the canon and its innovators through history. The buildings he looked at in some detail were the temple of Apollo at Thermon, Philo's Arsenal at Piraeus, Bramante's Tempietto, Michelangelo's Port Pia, Maderno's Sta Susanna, Bernini's Sant' Andrea al Quirinale, and Borromini's Roman Oratory. Secondly, again following in the tradition of architectural treatises stemming from Vitruvius, Smith presented the rules governing the use of the five orders, illustrating his points with his own drawings. Here he gave advice on the character and appropriate use of each column, historical examples of the types of variations which occurred, and methods for the geometrical construction of the details, such as the curvature of column shafts (entasis) and the spiral of the Ionic volute.

While he was at work on his own book it became increasingly clear to Smith that Vitruvius's treatise, the basis for all later architectural treatises, was very poorly understood. He therefore turned his attention to ancient buildings, especially those of the Hellenistic period to which Vitruvius had referred. He secured a second grant from the Graham to document these buildings with a view to writing a modern commentary on Vitruvius from the perspective of a practising architect. His growing interest in archaeological reconstructions led him to set students at both UIC and Yale the task of reconstructing Philo's Arsenal by using the contractor's specifications inscribed on a marble slab which had been found in 1882. His studies brought him into contact with Lothar Haselberger, the young German archaeologist who in 1979 had discovered inscriptions at the temple of Apollo at Didyma showing the profiles of the column base mouldings and a method for calculating the entasis of the columns. As an archaeologist who had initially trained as an architect himself, Haselberger was rather excited to find that his discoveries were not only of interest to his archaeological colleagues, but to practising architects also. In responding to Smith's enquiries about visiting Didyma, he wrote that he was "very much looking forward to study[ing] the temple with you" adding that he was "indeed ... pleased to be able to help link ancient and modern architecture."[4]

The realisation that major archaeological discoveries were still occurring had a profound impact on Smith. Throughout the classical tradition, architects had enriched their buildings by drawing on the latest archaeological finds: in fact before archaeology became a separate discipline in the later nineteenth century it was often the architects themselves who had made the discoveries. For example, Palladio had surveyed the ancient Roman baths and developed characteristically thermal spaces in his own villas; James "Athenian" Stuart was the first to record and publish Hellenistic buildings in Athens such as the Choragic Monument of Lysicrates, and subsequently used it in his own work at Spencer House; and C.R Cockerell was the first to publish the Temple of Apollo Epicurius at Bassae, and used its distinctive flared Ionic order in his Taylorian Institute in Oxford. By incorporating the latest discoveries in his own work, Smith demonstrated that classical architecture was capable of renewing itself now in just the same way as it always had since the Renaissance. He therefore used a method to calculate the entasis for the columns of his Vitruvian House that had been rediscovered by Haselberger and which had probably not been used for at least two millennia.

Smith's growing interest in Vitruvius had led him in 1981 to collaborate with a classicist from the University of California at Los Angeles, Ingrid Rowland, on a new edition of *De architectura*. Rowland was to translate the text afresh and Smith would provide a commentary for contemporary architects illustrated by his own interpretative drawings. He took a trip to turkey to study the Hellenistic buildings which had inspired Vitruvius. Smith was, of course, not the first architect to attempt an edition of Vitruvius. It is of interest that he inverted the process familiar from architects such as Palladio or Perrault, who had worked first on producing a new edition of Vitruvius and only subsequently wrote their own treatises. Smith, on the other hand, came to see the value of reinterpreting Vitruvius only while writing his own book. As the project developed, however, the collaboration became unfeasible. Rowland has published her new translation with illustrations by Thomas Noble Howe. Smith's interpretative work has been published on its own with support by the I.A. O'Shaughnessy foundation.[5]

Reconstruction of Vitruvius' Basilica at Fano, view of interior

Teaching

Rather surprisingly, Smith's first major teaching experience was at the Southern California Institute of Architecture, SCI-Arc, at the invitation of Michael Rotondi, Eric Owen Moss and Tom Mayne. Over the last two decades, SCI-Arc, an independent school of architecture in Los Angeles, has vigorously promoted its position as one of the most avant garde educational institutions in the United States. In 1983, when Smith was asked to teach a studio, SCI-Arc was heavily involved in the development and dissemination of Deconstructionism. Smith chose to set his students two design projects taken from real life: the first was a four week studio to design the Vatican pavilion at the New Orleans Fair, and the second devoted eight weeks to a proposed new Center for Decorative and Renaissance Art for the Getty Museum in Malibu, a commission which was subsequently expanded to encompass an entirely new museum, eventually to be realised by Richard Meier. This was the first design studio Smith had taught, and he made little attempt to impose a classical approach on the students; it was therefore hardly surprising that none of them pursued a traditional solution. As a result, Smith found himself being criticised for not being more rigorous by Eric Owen Moss, a faculty member who had clearly hoped that an enforced classical project would have sparked some debate within the school. It was precisely this same desire to stimulate conflict which resulted in Stanley Tigerman inviting Smith the following year to teach at the University of Illinois at Chicago, a large state school close to the Loop in downtown Chicago.

Tigerman had been involved with the school at UIC since 1964 and, despite a self-imposed nine-year hiatus in his teaching there, by 1984 he was in charge of a new one year Masters programme. He structured the curriculum of his course so that the students would take their first semester with a Deconstructionist and their second with a Classicist, leaving Tigerman himself to try to pick up the pieces. In an interview a few years later, Tigerman described the arrangement as follows: "So we'll have Eisenman, the deconstructionist, and Thomas Gordon Smith, the classicist, beating up on one another. What I want is to give the kids a real choice of the polar opposites of the classical language and … the deconstruction of the classical language."[6] He insisted that Smith should teach exactly what he wanted and that he would take the role of Smith's teaching assistant in the studio. Smith set four consecutive projects in his studio, and demonstrated that he had learned the lesson from SCI-Arc that contemporary projects would not easily persuade students to engage wholeheartedly with the principles of classical design. The first three assignments were archaeological reconstructions, essentially in the Beaux-Arts tradition of the *envoi*: Philo's Arsenal at Peiraeus, Pliny the Younger's Tuscan Villa, and a sixteenth-century pavilion at Genazzano, near Palestrina. In each case the type of evidence from which the students would be working was different: a set of contractor's specifications, a literary description, and ruinous remains. The three short exercises introduced the students sequentially to the rudiments of each of the main orders, Doric, Ionic and Corinthian, and to the architecture of three different periods, Greek, Roman and Renaissance. For the final project, Smith set them to design a chapel to be added to Frank Lloyd Wright's Charnley House, a rather uncharacteristically classical early work of the master which would require them to apply the understanding of the orders which they had just acquired. This same semester Smith was also teaching again in Southern California, but this time at the University of California at Los Angeles where Charles Moore was then a professor. Smith taught a class there on "Rendering the Classical Orders," a course which he ensured was also offered by the San Francisco Architecture Club.

Two years later, in the Spring of 1986, Thomas Beeby invited Smith to teach a studio at the School of

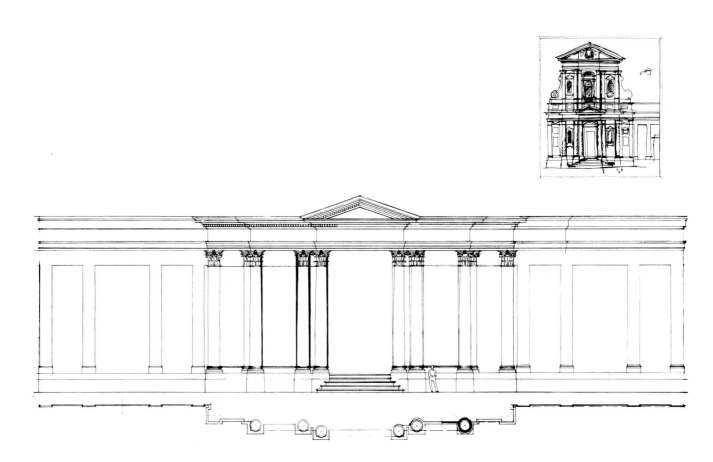

Measured drawing of Sta Susanna, Rome

Architecture at Yale University. Beeby had been director of the school at UIC when Smith had taught there and was now dean at Yale. Smith called the course "Problems in Classical Architecture as a Medium for Contemporary Architecture" and set his students similar projects to those at UIC: Philo's Arsenal, Pliny's Laurentian Villa, and an addition of a recital hall and exhibition space for the Yale Collection of Musical Instruments. Again, the first two exercises introduced the students to the rudiments of classical design, which would then be applied in the last project. Smith chose the Collection of Musical Instruments because it allowed him to introduce a theme which had increasingly interested him since he had taken up the harpsichord in 1984: the application of harmonic proportions to architecture. Since the discovery that the musical scale could be broken down into numerical ratios, supposedly made by the sixth-century BC Greek philosopher Pythagoras, architects had applied these

ratios to the design of buildings. In the Renaissance, interest in the application of these harmonic proportions was revived, in particular by Italian theorists and practitioners such as Palladio.[7] Smith had examined this concept in a series of lectures he had organised the previous year at the San Francisco Architecture Club, and was now exploring its possible application in contemporary buildings. For the reviews of the studio, Smith took full advantage of the presence in the Art History department at Yale of Jerome Pollit, one of the most distinguished historians of Greek architecture. The fact that it was a rare occurrence for Professor Pollit to be invited to the school of architecture as a critic is clear from his enthusiastic letter of thanks to Smith: "Your session on Philo's warehouse was, quite honestly, one of the high points of the current term for me . . . I would really like to see what the students did with Pliny's villa.[8] In these student exercises which were making a genuine

Carlos Martinez, student project for the addition of a chapel to the Charnley House, Chicago

contribution to the understanding of ancient architecture it might seem that Smith was finally taking Claude Stoller's remark of dozen years earlier to heart: "So you want to be an applied archaeologist?"

Stanley Tigerman had clearly been pleased with the results of Smith's teaching at UIC and invited him to take a full-time tenure track position on the faculty when he became Head of the School of Architecture in 1986. Looking back, on the occasion of a critical report from the National Architectural Accrediting Board five years later, Tigerman explained his philosophy: "The intention, of course, was to bring the issues of the day into the studio ... and in so doing, to bring these issues into direct confrontation with equally valuable, albeit traditionally derived values ... To best represent these traditions, Thomas Gordon Smith was hired. ... The juxtaposition of these two attitudes was intended, so as to offer the students the ultimate choice to establish his or her own direction. I

have always believed that the student is, appropriately, in the best position to make choices, and that it is the faculty's obligation to bring the fullest plate of offerings to the table in order to facilitate student choice."[9]

Despite the fact that Smith had only recently completed the house in Richmond for his family that he had been waiting to build for nearly a decade, he accepted the offer. He had been having great difficulty finding work for his practice in San Francisco, and was especially disillusioned having seen promising large scale projects, such as the Edgewood Center, come to nothing. It seems ironic that as the prospects for a classical revival emerging from post-modernism were crushed by the growing fashion for deconstruction, Smith should find himself rescued from his languishing classical practice by deconstructionist schools. In retrospect, he valued both the difficult time in practice and the challenging environments of these schools, for forcing him to acquire that rigour which Vitruvius had referred to as *auctoritas*. [Note comment re Moore and SFbay area - also new wave decon in bay area]

As it transpired, Smith only spent three years at UIC though during that time a great deal was achieved. He and Tigerman recruited a number of adjunct faculty with classical leanings: Thomas Rajkovich who won a competition with David Mayernik for a $20 million project for the Capitol Grounds in Saint Paul, Minnesota; John Tittmann who had been one of Smith's star students at Yale; and Hans Baldauf, whom Smith had previously hired in California to help him on his book. In addition to teaching the studios required of him, Smith launched a Programme for Vitruvian Studies, for which he organised colloquia on "Rule and Invention in Vitruvius" and "Vitruvius and the Big Idea" featuring such distinguished archaeologists as J.J. Coulton, William Macdonald and Lothar Haselberger. Coursework for his students ranged widely, from field trips to a limestone quarry and traditional stone mason's yard in Bloomington, Indiana, through quizzes where they had to identify the elements of the classical orders such as guttae, to a six-week design studio for a high rise on Michigan Avenue which would respond sympathetically to the Beaux-Arts classicism of Shepley, Rutan and Coolidge's Art Institute (1893) and other neighbouring facades.

The University of Notre Dame, a rich private Catholic university in South Bend, Indiana, was warned by the National Architectural Accrediting Board in 1988 that its school of architecture was in danger of being placed on probation for its professional accreditation. The university authorities were not only keen to avoid this potentially disastrous situation, but were also open to the suggestion of the programme being completely revised and given a new focus. Smith, whose Catholic faith helped make him an ideal candidate, was invited to become the new Chairman of the school in 1989. Once there, he set about the total reform of the school. While a few of the existing professors were sympathetic to classicism, for instance the theorist Norman Crowe and historian John Stamper, most were not; Smith therefore hired

new faculty and added four full-time professors, the most notable of whom were the Greek-Americans Michael Lykoudis and Richard Economakis, the Lebanese-American Samir Younès, and a fellow Catholic, Duncan Stroik. There were also other aspects of the existing programme which helped smooth the transformation. A mandatory year of study in Rome, which had been required of all third-year architecture students since 1969, not only ensured that students visited and measured the remains of ancient classical buildings, but also gave them first hand experience of addressing contemporary design problems in historic urban sites.

As we have seen, Smith attached a great deal of importance to the role of the treatise in the transmission and development of classicism, and consequently he embarked on a programme of acquisitions for the library, raising funds to buy some five hundred rare books, mostly classical treatises and early American patternbooks. He also helped raised the funds for the complete refurbishment of the school's building and took the leading role in a collaboration with the campus architects to design its extension and restoration. He continued to organise colloquia on Vitruvius at South Bend, thus extending the six-year long series of events that he had previously arranged in Los Angeles, San Francisco and Chicago. In collaboration with the faculty, the existing undergraduate programme was overhauled to give students a rigorous training in Classicism and other programmes were introduced, most notably an accredited Master's course and a variety of overseas studios, such as one which was held jointly in St Petersburg with the only other classical schools in the world, The Prince of Wales's Institute of Architecture and the Russian Academy of the Fine Arts. The school, which had previously been just a department in the College of Engineering, was made autonomous for the first time, When he came to step down as Chairman after nine years, in 1998, the new curriculum was flourishing to the extent that over thirty architectural offices from all over the country were sending representatives to the careers day at school in order to compete for graduates.

Rare books were not the only objects that Smith began to hunt down once he was settled at Notre Dame. The simple classical furniture of the second quarter of the nineteenth century, known now as "Empire" but then described as either "plain style" or "Grecian," also appealed to him and he began to collect pieces for the house he was intending to build for his family in South Bend. As he conducted research on the sofas, chairs and tables he was finding, these two interests in books and furniture came together. He discovered that many of the furniture designs were clearly derived from cabinet makers' patternbooks in much the same way as architectural books were disseminating the new Greek Revival style at this time. Smith's research resulted in him preparing introductions to reprints of books by two authors: Thomas King, a British furniture draughtsman, publisher and upholsterer, and Asher Benjamin, the first American to compile an architectural book. King was responsible for as many as twenty-eight separate books, evenly divided between furniture designs, which covered the Grecian, Gothic, Rococo and Elizabethan styles, and drapery patterns. The book which Smith suggested to the publisher, Dover, that they should reprint was King's most popular title, *The Modern Style of Cabinet Work Exemplified* of 1829, which bar a few gothic designs was almost exclusively devoted to the Grecian Style. In his introduction Smith voiced the hope that, "combined with many other impulses in contemporary society, this reprint could well contribute to the revival of classical forms and principles in our built environment."[10] To show that he was not being over-optimistic he accompanied this with a photograph of the Klismos chair with a splat derived from an Aeolic capital which he had designed in collaboration with its maker, Robert Brandt. Similarly, in his introduction to the reprint of Benjamin's *Practice of Architecture* (1833) and *The Builder's Guide* (1839), two of the most influential works in the popularisation of the Grecian style in

American architecture, Smith explained that in addition to the general reader interested in Americana, the historian and the preservationist, this reprint was geared towards the practising architect. By way of encouragement he illustrated four modern buildings in this idiom: John B. Tittmann's house in Concord, Massachusetts; Stephen Falatko's Residence at Carpenter Hill, Stanford, New York; Allan Greenberg's News Building, Athens, Georgia; and the house Smith himself designed for his parents-in-law in Livermore, California.

With a research fellowship from the Winterthur Museum in Delaware, Smith spent the summer of 1994 continuing to work in the same vein. He wrote a substantial historical introduction for a single-volume reprint of three books published in Baltimore in 1840 by the English immigrant John Hall: *The Cabinet Makers' Assistant*; *A Series of Select, Original and Modern Designs for Dwelling Houses*; and *A New and Concise Method of Handrailing*.[11] Here, however, he stopped short of making reference to the contemporary revival of classicism in which he was so intimately involved. Nevertheless, the unexplained inclusion in this volume of the frankly obscure *Method of Handrailing*, which Hall had published primarily to explain how to use his own bizarre invention of the concentric ellipsograph, was for the simple reason that Smith had himself found it useful in designing the staircase for the Kulb House in Illinois.

In the summer of 1995 a fellowship from the Philadelphia Athenaeum enabled Smith to work on the relationship between Grecian furniture and architecture in Philadelphia in the 1830s, a time when it was relinquishing to New York its pre-eminence as the first city in the United States.

At the same time he also began to research a unique case study, the 1840s construction of Millford plantation in South Carolina and its complete furnishing by Duncan Phyfe.[12]

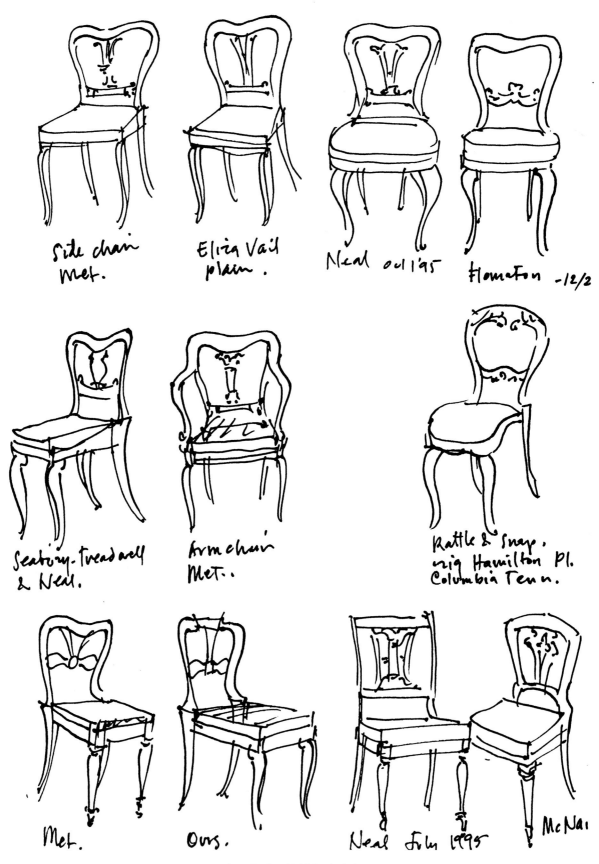

side chair
Met.

Eliza Vail
plain.

Neal oct 1'95

Flomaton -12/2

Seatury. Treadwell
& Neal.

Armchair
Met..

Rattle & Snap.
1819 Hamilton Pl.
Columbia Tenn.

Met.

Ours.

Neal July 1995

McNai

above: Studies of "plain" style chairs

opposite: Klismos Chair, designed with Robert Brandt, 1993

CHAPTER VI

Mature Work I: Houses

"I'd rather meet with tardy genius than
punctual mediocrity any day"
Daniel Weeks

The Vitruvian House

opposite: Vitruvian House, South Bend, detail of Ionic capital

above: Vitruvian House, South Bend, detail of metope

Following his appointment as chairman of the school of architecture at the University of Notre Dame, Smith set about finding a suitable site in South Bend to build a house for his large family. Marika found a lot which was just two miles east of the campus, at the end of a cul-de-sac in a conventional suburban subdivision. The site was slightly wooded, ensuring that even when viewed from a short distance the house would be seen in isolation – a clear advantage over the extremely narrow lot on which he had built the Richmond Hill House.

Keen that the design of his house should be rooted in local traditions, Smith and his wife took a trip to Ann Arbor, Michigan, to look at examples of Greek Revival houses dating from the 1840s. This choice of precedent was also stimulated by the desire to have an appropriate setting for the collection of antique furniture that Smith had started to assemble on arrival at Notre Dame. He adapted the basic Greek Revival type of a two-storey Ionic block flanked by single-storey Doric wings by enriching it with all his previous interests: a Vitruvian module for the portico, a Baroque oval plan for the dining room, a Palladian cruciform volume for the Oecus, a complex iconographic programme in fresco, and, though muted to suit the Mid West, polychromy tying it all together. Even his most recent interest in the "plain style" furniture of Duncan Phyfe surfaced in the design of the kitchen where cabinet

above: Vitruvian House, South Bend, façade

opposite: Vitruvian House, South Bend, view of oecus towards fireplace

doors are framed by Phyfe's distinctive scrolls. Unlike the Richmond Hill House, the budget did not require the use of architectural salvage; however, considerations of economy did result in the terrazzo copy of the floor of the San Francisco Stock Exchange for the Oecus being reconsidered after an estimate of $27,000.

The house's central portico in antis consists of a pair of Ionic columns in Indiana limestone, arranged according to the Vitruvian proportions for the eustylos, or well-columned, disposition. Their ratio of column diameter to intercolumniation is 1:2.25, and of diameter to height is 1:9.5. The profile of their bases and the entasis of their shafts were designed in accordance with the discoveries by Haselberger at Didyma. Similarly, the three fasciae of the epistylium or architrave each slope at a different angle imitating an effect which Smith observed himself at the Temple of Artemis at Magnesia by Hermogenes. The result is that the architrave has a lively, slightly bulging profile which perfectly conveys the sense of the weight of the roof being transferred to the columns. The uppermost fascia of the architrave bears the simple inscription: VITRUVIAN HOUSE ANNO MCMXC. The opening is flanked on either side by bays of buff Roman bricks. Each bay is framed by a pair of brick pilasters terminated by a stone cyma reversa abacus, creating, overall, a hexastylos portico to support the pediment. A central terracotta acroterion surmounts the apex. The low Doric wings are built of coarse red concrete blocks to contrast with the fine Roman bricks of the central block. Each wing is articulated by pilasters to create five bays – three wide bays in the middle, the outer two of which are windows, and a narrow one at each end. These stripped pilasters support a plain architrave of buff bricks and a polychrome triglyph frieze above.

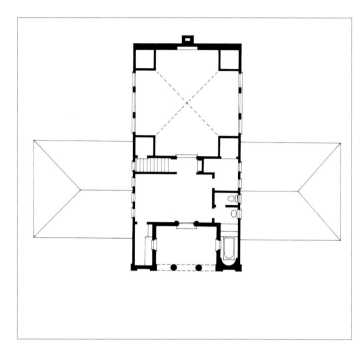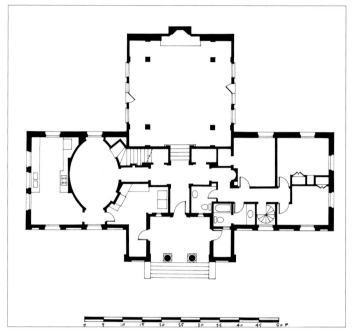

above: Vitruvian House, South Bend, plan

opposite: Vitruvian House, South Bend, oecus towards entrance

Here, the triglyphs are of blue-black Norman bricks set vertically to frame metopes which illustrate the Labours of Hercules. Each labour has three metopes devoted to it, the first of which depicts in low relief the skull of the animal the hero vanquished. The whole house stands on a rusticated basement, consisting of alternating bands of stone and Roman brick in the central pavilion and rough bricks and blocks at the sides.

The main entrance is framed by a Doric door case with a triglyph frieze in contrasting light and dark wood. One enters a hall in the form of a Greek cross which leads down a short flight of steps into the main living room of the house, called an Oecus after Vitruvius. This dramatically scaled room is twenty-four feet square, with intersecting barrel vaults inspired by the salone of Palladio's Villa Foscari. This cross-vault springs from four abstracted Corinthian piers in the same manner as that of the androne of Palladio's Palazzo Porto in Vicenza and rises to a height of twenty-two feet. The room is overlooked from above the entrance by a balcony, the balustrade of which is copied from a window guard in a Grecian farmhouse in Michigan. The hearth is in axis with the hall and is set in a shallow niche eight feet high, lined with trompe l'oeil Delft tiles painted with the birds of Northern Indiana and housing a Rumford fireplace. The cross axis is terminated by large French windows below with thermal windows above following the form of the vault. The vault itself is frescoed with a programme illustrating the eight most influential architects in Smith's personal pantheon with their most supportive patrons: Pytheos with Alexander, Kallimachus with Pericles, Agrippa with Augustus, Apollodorus with Trajan, Palladio with Daniele Barbaro, Michelangelo with Pope Paul III, Bernini with Pope Alexander VII, and Borromini with Pope Innocent X. The presence of their patrons is a crucial acknowledgement of the importance of the enlightened client in the creation of great architecture. This theme is taken further in the four tableaux painted on the vault depicting Hadrian being dismissed by Trajan and Apollodorus,[1] Vitruvius presenting his design for the Basilica at Fano to Augustus, Palladio drawing in the ruins of the Baths of Caracalla, and Borromini and Bernini debating the details of Doric architecture. The whole composition is dominated by the magisterial figure of Architettura above the hearth, who is flanked by Vitruvius and Deinocrates, representing decorum and ingenium;

above: Vitruvian House, South Bend, dining room view towards hall

opposite: Vitruvian House, South Bend, dining room view towards window

Vitruvian House, South Bend, oecus ceiling from below

these ancient architects are matched on the opposite wall by twentieth century ones, Maybeck and Plecnik, whose careful balancing of rule and invention is shown in a selection of their buildings on either side of the balcony. In the frieze of the entablature from which the vault springs is an inscription from Vitruvius (I, i, 2) translated by Ingrid Rowland:

> Architects who have tried to obtain manual
> skill but no education have never been able
> to muster an authority equal to the quality
> of their work. Conversely, those who depend
> only on calculations and writing seem to
> have chased after a shadow, not the real thing.
> But those who have mastered both skills –

endowed, if you will, with a full arsenal –
these have reached their goal quickly and
with authority.

The transverse corridor of the cruciform hall leads from a niche, which conceals the passage into the children's bedrooms on the ground floor, to the oval dining room. Here, one wall features a roof-top panorama of Rome painted by Ruth Englehardt Stroik, the wife of one of the new faculty members recruited by Smith to Notre Dame. The ceiling is tented with fabric, creating the impression of dining in a temporary kiosk on the roof of a Roman Palazzo. The entrance to the dining room is flanked to one side by a niche and to the other by the doorway to the stairs leading up to the

above left: Vitruvian House, South Bend, oecus fresco, detail of Pope Paul III and Michelangelo

above right: Vitruvian House, South Bend, Smith executing the fresco

main bedroom. Beyond the dining room is a kitchen and breakfast area. In addition to concealing the main staircase, poché is skilfully used to accommodate utility areas, cloak rooms and wardrobes. The basement floor also has bedrooms and a den. The ensemble is com-pleted by a shed in the garden painted and ornamented to look like a small polychrome temple or shrine.

Smith intended this house to be far more than an attractive and convenient residence for his large family. His intentions in the iconographic programme are easily interpreted: the Labours of Hercules signify his own commitment to executing the difficult tasks he knew lay ahead in transforming the school, and the cycle of his architectural and intellectual heroes in the

Oecus retrace the path of his own development as an architect and theorist. On a less explicit level, other layers of significance can be divined in the house. First, it drew together with impressive ease – one might even say *sprezzatura* – all those themes and interests which Smith had explored during the past fifteen years; secondly, it allowed him to apply in practice his scholarly study of the text of Vitruvius; and, finally, and perhaps most importantly, it helped him resolve the direction he wished to pursue in his architecture in the future: a literate application of classicism, drawing freely on the entire twenty-five centuries of tradition, that is at once both rich and rigorous, balancing rule and invention, and which above all demonstrates its ample suitability for contemporary life.

The Wilson House

opposite: Wilson House, Livermore, door from atrium

above: Wilson House, Livermore, detail of capital

While Smith did not operate a fully-staffed office in South Bend, over the next eight years he had a number of opportunities to put into practice this approach in both private and public commissions. The first of these was a house for Marika's parents in Livermore, California. While a Greek Revival idiom was clearly suitable for the mid West, on account of the extensive adoption of the style in the early nineteenth century, it might seem less appropriate in Northern California. However, Marika's mother, Demetra Corombus Wilson, was of Greek origin, and so Smith chose a Grecian theme, looking in particular for inspiration at the Tower of the Winds, a Hellenistic monument in the Athenian Agora which housed a timekeeping device. Despite its late date and small scale it had enjoyed widespread popularity since it had first been made famous by Stuart and Revett's publication of *The Antiquities of Athens* in 1762. The single-storey Wilson house presents a severely symmetrical and windowless façade to the street. A small pedimented porch of two Indiana limestone columns with carved Pergamene capitals after those of the Tower of the Winds is balanced on either side by symmetrical garage doors. This theme is continued in the octagonal lantern, each external face of which has a terracotta version of the appropriate wind and its name in Greek. These names, Notus for South, Boreas for North, etc., were even used on the drawings submitted to the local planning authority, who were additionally confused by the designation of rooms as cubiculum, magistrale or coquinia. The entrance, between a pair of symmetrical garage doors, leads immediately into a small Tuscan courtyard modelled on the impluvium of an ancient villa and proportioned according to Vitruvius's recommendations. From the foyer, one gains access to the Oecus, which runs north-south virtually the whole length of the main house. In order to maintain harmonious proportions in relation to its length, its ceiling is considerably higher than the rooms to either side, and the room is divided into separate dining and living areas by a pair of columns. At its north end it is lit by the octagonal lantern above, while the entire south wall is filled by a thermal window which is articulated externally by Doric piers supporting a triglyph frieze.

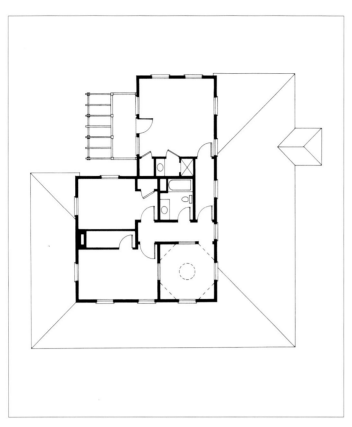

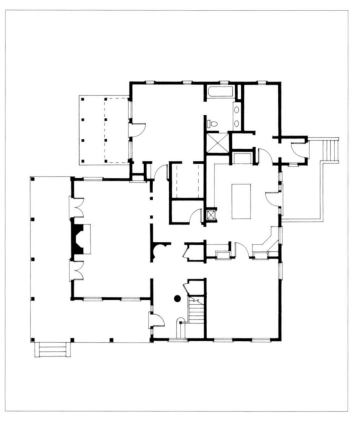

above left: Wilson House, Livermore, plan

above right: Grecian House, Greensboro, plan

below: Wilson House, Livermore, exterior from road

opposite: Wilson House, Livermore, Cupola

Country Home House

Earlier this century, women's magazines played a key role in popularising avant garde approaches to house design. Frank Lloyd Wright's Prairie Style, for instance, was widely promulgated through the publication of his scheme for a $1,000 house for the *Ladies Home Journal*. Today, glossy middlebrow periodicals are playing a similar role in the revival of traditional approaches to design: in the United Kingdom, despite the existence of a thriving architectural press, the magazine *Country Life* has been almost the only supporter of contemporary classical work by architects such as Quinlan Terry and John Simpson. In 1995, the American lifestyle magazine *Country Home*, responded to a request from a reader about how to go about commissioning an architect, by deciding to follow in the footsteps of the *Ladies Home Journal*. The result was a series of articles chronicling the whole process of building a new home from selecting an architect through to the final decorating and furnishing of the finished house for the benefit of its readers.

The brief was clearly targeted to appeal to *Country Home*'s readership: the charm and elegance of a nineteenth century farmhouse, but with all the technological conveniences of a late twentieth-century suburban home. In looking for an architect, Dan Weeks, the editor responsible for the project, described their ideal as "an architect who can improvise as would a jazz musician, combining familiar patterns with delightful invention, naturally and seamlessly."[2] With his experience of designing handsome domestic buildings on a tight budget and his recent studies of

Greek revival architecture, Smith was the ideal choice. His solution for a site in Greensboro, North Carolina, was to wrap a simple one-storey porch around a double height Palladian pavilion. Rather than facing the street, the main entrance leads sideways off this porch into a surprisingly grand staircase hall which rises the full height of the house to an octagonal ceiling with a central oculus. Despite the low-key, informal exterior, classical detail abounds inside, sometimes rather quirkily interpreted by the builder in much the same way as one often finds in historic vernacular buildings. A sixteen-sided Corinthian column provides structural support in the hall, six guttae depend from each tread of the oak [poplar?] staircase, and doors and windows have battered Greek revival frames. The handsomely proportioned living room is dominated by an authentically overscaled Rumford fireplace. Throughout the year-long project Daniel Weeks was hugely impressed by the whole process of being Smith's "client." He described how he had been waiting to collect Smith at the airport, only to discover that the architect had missed his plane. It transpired that while Smith was waiting in the departure lounge for the boarding call, an improvement in the design occurred to him, so he unrolled the drawings and started working on them there and then. He became so engrossed in developing the idea that he didn't hear the boarding call being announced and missed the plane. Far from being upset by this absentmindedness, Weeks commented that "I'd rather meet with tardy genius than punctual mediocrity any day."[3]

The Kulb House

Following the publication of an article on the Vitruvian House in the Notre Dame alumni magazine, Smith was approached by a couple who had close connections with the university. They owned a seven-acre site not far away in Illinois, and wanted to build a traditional house of rather exceptional character. The setting for the 10,000 square foot house was a meadow, flanked by ravines sloping northwards to a lake. Smith took his inspiration from the mid-Western interpretations of the Greek Revival built by prosperous farmers and merchants from 1840. In particular he considered the Swift house in Vermilion, Ohio, sadly demolished in the 1920s, which Smith attributes to Minard Lafever.

The Kulb house faces south to take advantage of the natural topography of the site; this orientation allows the entrance to the main floor to be on grade, while to the rear a basement storey is excavated for garages, utility rooms and a family room to the North. The Indiana limestone of the portico in antis contrast strongly with the Roman bricks of the body of the house. The order of the portico is derived from the temple on the river Illyssus, as published by Stuart and Revett in *The Antiquities of Athens*. The limestone blocks of the antae are specially cut to be exactly the same size as the surrounding bricks, thus heightening the contrast between the different materials by making their modules identical. Within, a freestanding spiral staircase dominates the forty-five foot high hall. Here Smith was inspired by an extraordinarily fine staircase designed by the Baltimore builder-architect, Francis

Costigan, for his Shrewsbury House, Madison, Indiana, of 1848. To assist in its construction Smith used a work published in Baltimore which was probably known to Costigan, John Hall's *Method of Handrailing* of 1840. Looking directly through this hall, beyond the stairs, is the entrance to the double height Oecus, or living room, which extends to the rear of the house. This doorway rises the full height of the room and is derived from a Greek source: the Temple of Apollo at Didyma. Incorporated into the architrave above the door is a frieze pierced with a running anthemion motif which is the air return grille. It is a perfect example of how the mouldings and other details of the classical language can be adapted to accommodate the latest technology unobtrusively. As one enters the oecus, the impressive sense of scale established in the hall is maintained by full length windows on either side, giving views of the lake, and culminating in a Serliana window at the far end of the room. The draperies for this room were also specified by Smith, who modelled them on an example published by the British furniture designer and curtain manufacturer, Thomas King, in *The Upholsterers' Accelerator* of 1833.

The grand scale of this room indicates the semi-public nature of a house intended to be used extensively for entertaining. This formal articulation continues in the dining room and sitting room to either side of the entrance hall. These contrast with the rather more private realm of the main bedroom suite located on the ground floor beyond the sitting room. This suite

Thomas Gordon Smith

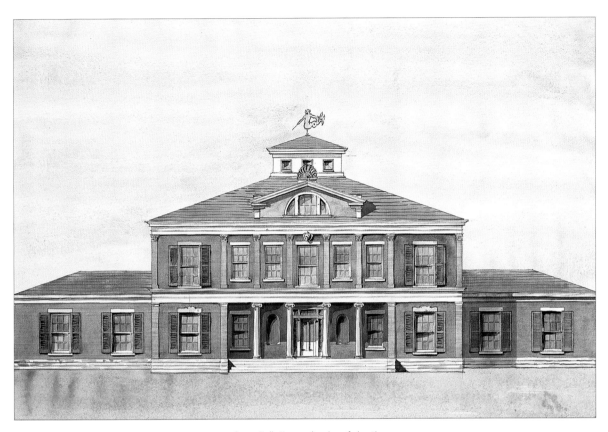

above: Kulb House, drawing of elevation

below: Kulb house, façade

opposite: Kulb house, south façade

above: Kulb House, detail

below: Kulb house, detail of portico

opposite: Kulb house, façade

above and opposite: Kulb House, interiors

occupies the single-storey wing to the East of the house, which balances the kitchen wing to the West. The second floor is devoted to children's bedrooms and a playroom. The most withdrawn and private space of the house is in the attic, a study which is illuminated by a thermal window set in a large dormer over the portico. The roofscape is further enlivened by a square lantern with weather vane which lights the stairhall.

In marked contrast to the isolated rural site of the Kulb residence, the house Smith designed for Terrence and Margie Johnson was for a relatively narrow urban lot in Chicago. This enabled him to draw on his studies of Greek Revival town house design, for instance John Hall in his *Series of Select, Original and Modern Designs for Dwelling Houses* provided a number of examples of

the type of compact planning that Smith was to adopt in this house. On the ground floor, no space is wasted in redundant circulation areas, with all the rooms wrapped around a central service core. On entering the foyer one is either led directly to a freestanding spiral staircase beyond which lies the family room, or into the parlour, the gently-curving window of which occupies the central bay of the street façade. At the back of the house, the kitchen lies between the family room and the octagonal breakfast room, from which one can gain access to the garage via a mudroom. Externally, the ground floor is finished in a warm buff limestone, with brick and stone dressings above.

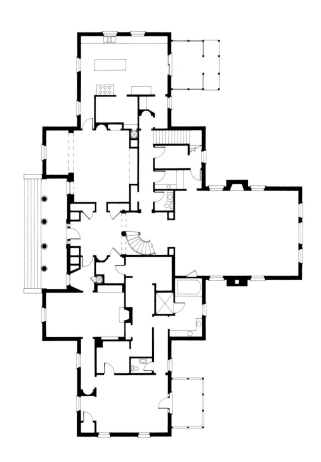
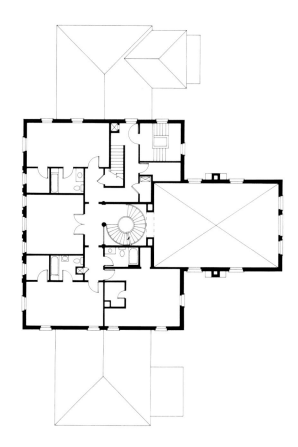

above: Kulb House, plans

below: Kulb House, interior

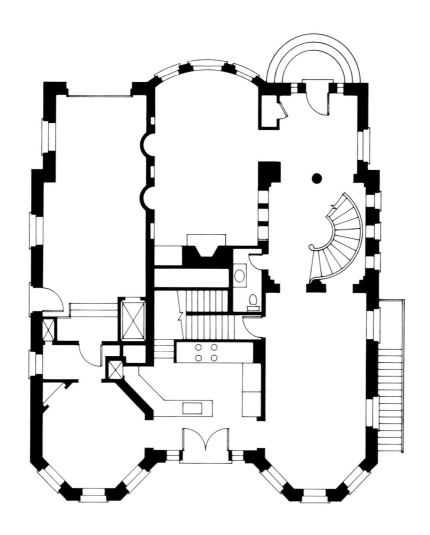

above: Johnson House, Chicago, plan of ground floor

below: Johnson House, Chicago, colour perspective

above: Frame for El Greco's Assumption of the Virgin, *The Art Institute, before gilding*

opposite: Frame for El Greco's Assumption of the Virgin, *The Art Institute, Working drawings for composition mouldings*

CHAPTER VII

Mature Work II: Public Buildings

"The only [architect] with the sensitivity and … the dedication for your kind of work would be … Thomas Gordon Smith … you must meet with him to see if … the direction his designs are taking would be pleasing to you or not. Personally, I like them very much"

Philip Johnson

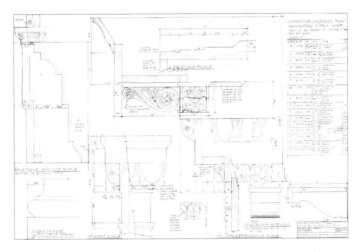

Having moved to Chicago, the first commission Smith received in the city was not for a building, but a for a picture frame. Put so baldly, this might seem rather too minor a project for consideration here, but the picture in question was El Greco's *Assumption of the Virgin* in The Art Institute. It was painted in the late 1570s as part of a large altarpiece for the Bernardine convent of Santo Domingo el Antiguo in Toledo, which had been designed in part by Juan de Herrera, the architect of Philip II's palace-monastery, the Escorial. The ensemble of paintings making up the altarpiece, which included a *Holy Trinity* and an image of Veronica's Veil, was broken up in 1827 when the *Assumption* was sold and, after passing through several hands, it was finally purchased by the Art Institute in 1906. At that time a new frame was commissioned from a Boston frame designer, but like its early nineteenth-century predecessor, this revealed strips of canvas which had been added to the original image. When the institute refurbished its Galleries of European Art in 1987, they commissioned Smith to design a new

frame that would allow the picture to be appreciated in something approaching its original setting. The result elevates the painting dramatically to seven feet above the floor and conceals the later canvas additions by using the Fornix motif of an arch flanked by columns to frame the image. A projecting base, painted in faux marble, simulates the effect of an altar table, while the entire frame was gilded in imitation of the original sixteenth-century altarpiece. Smith's knowledge of the practical application of classicism in contemporary building enabled him to considerably reduce the cost of construction; instead of every detail being carved by hand, Smith was able to specify much of the cornice, frieze and architrave in his working drawings using composition mouldings which while easily available would nevertheless be correct in both form and proportions. The Art Institute donors who paid for the new frame, Gerald and Jane Gidwitz, were clearly pleased with the result of their beneficence as Jane immediately commissioned sketch designs from Smith for the possible remodelling of their Chicago apartment.

The Norman Rockwell Museum

opposite: Norman Rockwell Museum, Stockbridge, Four Freedoms gallery

above: Norman Rockwell Museum, Stockbridge, perspective view in landscape

One of the most popular of twentieth-century American painters, Norman Rockwell, left a substantial collection of paintings in order that a Museum devoted to his life and work might be created in his home town of Stockbridge, Massachusetts. In 1987, Smith was invited to take part with two other architectural firms, Robert A.M. Stern, and Hardy, Holzman and Pfeiffer, in a limited competition for the design of the museum. This project resulted in a surprising departure for Smith from the highly personal idiom familiar from his Californian projects. Here he chose a colonial Dutch-American style which he saw as appropriate to the vision of small-town America which characterized Rockwell's paintings. While this was his first attempt at this style, the result carried remarkable conviction, despite the difficult challenge Smith had

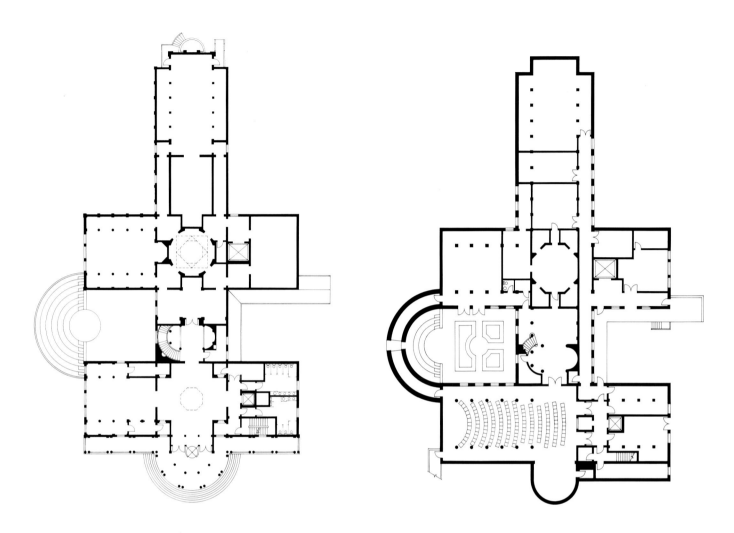

above left: Norman Rockwell Museum, Stockbridge, plan of ground floor

above right: Norman Rockwell Museum, Stockbridge, plan of basement floor

knowingly set himself by using an essentially domestic idiom for a public building. On the main entrance front, to the South, a hipped roof extends low over a porch of paired Tuscan columns running the entire length of the facade. In its centre the entrance is marked by a wide rotunda projecting forward from the building around which the porch is wrapped. The side elevations feature large gambrel gables, almost entirely filled by thermal windows; below these are three-light windows, the stone sills and mullions of which rise from the rusticated stone basement and contrast with the red brick walls. Above the expanse of the slate roof, rises an elegant wooden cupola with its own hipped roof in copper surmounted by a weather vane. Despite the lack of Smith's usual references to full-blooded antiquity, there were, however, still some personal

motifs, such as the Michelangelesque doorcase in the main foyer, where the pediment was not pierced by an opening, but filled by a clock.

Heinrich Klotz was one of the members of the jury convened to judge the competition. As one might expect knowing the unflagging support which Klotz had previously given Smith, on this occasion he argued vigorously for Smith's design and was nearly successful in persuading the other jurors. However, Stern's project, in a Greek Revival idiom, won their favour primarily on account of being partially buried in the hillside to give it a low profile and avoid monumentality. Following the announcement of the winner, Klotz wrote to Smith to commiserate with him. He lamented how close the decision had been and confessed that "afterwards I became quite melancholic and got drunk."[1]

above: Norman Rockwell Museum, Stockbridge, foyer

below: Norman Rockwell Museum, Stockbridge, south elevetion

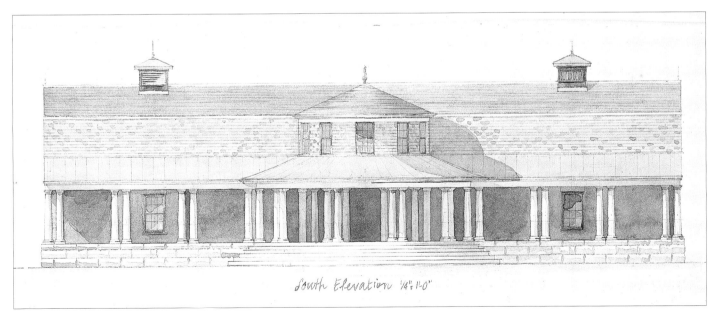

South Elevation ¼":1'-0"

School of Architecture, Notre Dame

In 1964 the department of architecture at Notre Dame moved into the Lemonnier Library, a handsome limestone building which had been built in 1917 by the New York architect Edward Tilton. The building is unusual on the Notre Dame campus for being constructed of stone in the Beaux Arts classicism of the American Renaissance while its neighbours are mostly gothic buildings of yellow brick. Though the library is externally noble, it was not well suited to its new role since most of the interior was designed to accommodate book stacks rather than architectural studios, and therefore provided only poorly lit and cramped working conditions. The inadequacy of the original building became painfully apparent as a result of Smith's expansion of the programme and his culminating achievement as chairman of the school was its extension and renovation. For this twelve million dollar project, Smith collaborated with Ellerbe Becket who were then the University's chosen architect for all new buildings on campus, and work began in Fall 1995 being completed in the Summer of 1997. The project was funded by a donation from a Notre Dame alumnus and his wife, William and Joanne Bond, after whom the new building was named. Bond had graduated from Notre Dame with a bachelor's degree in architecture in 1950 and returned to his home state of Tennessee to found an architectural and engineering firm in Memphis. This proved phenomenally successful in the field of hotel design, so that by the late 1960s the firm was designing between one and two hundred projects annually, mostly Holiday Inns, Ramada Inns, Sheraton Hotels, Howard Johnsons and Travelodges, but also office buildings, nursing homes and apartment complexes. A key to the firm's success was the development of an efficient computerized system to design buildings with similar specifications.

The new Bond Hall was some forty percent bigger than its predecessor and this increase in size, from fifty-one thousand square feet to over seventy thousand, enabled it to house the architecture library and rare books room, an auditorium, department and faculty offices, studios for undergraduates and graduates, computer laboratory, wood workshop, an exhibition gallery and a cafe.

The first scheme featured an ambitious apsed auditorium to the rear of the building, which was flanked by staircase towers terminated by octagonal Towers of the Winds. Budgetary constraints required that at a very late stage in the design process the extension was dramatically reduced in size. At great speed, Smith reworked his design so that the rear facade of the building was modified by omitting the apse. This still allowed for the insertion of two new staircases, the expansion of the studios, and the creation of a new rare books room lit by a large thermal window. The extension is executed in a buff brick, both for reasons of economy and to distinguish it from the limestone of the original building. In the centre of the new rear facade is a coat of arms, a bust of Vitruvius by Miklos Simon, and an inscription from his *De architectura* concerning the education of the architect. Vignolan brackets are used to create a cornice for the two staircase towers, while the Doric frieze of the central section features metope sculptures of bucrania and wreaths with architectural drawing instruments.

The heart of the renovated building is the Library's new reading room. This is dominated by four baseless Doric columns rising dramatically through two stories to support a skylight. Smaller reading rooms and balconies open off this central space, beyond which are further book stacks and the new rare book room. This last part of the program was needed because of Smith's vigorous acquisitions policy which had focussed on treatises on classical architecture and nineteenth century American patternbooks. To house the folios, Smith designed a large book press in the form of architectural frontispiece. Its superimposed orders are a physical realisation of the canons expounded in the treatises which lie within. This was built by Robert Brandt, with whom Smith had collaborated on a number of other pieces of furniture. The opening of the new building was celebrated with a degree ceremony at which, appropriately enough, three of Smith's fellow classical architects, Demetri Porphyrios, Elizabeth Plater-Zyberk, and Allan Greenberg, were given honorary doctorates.

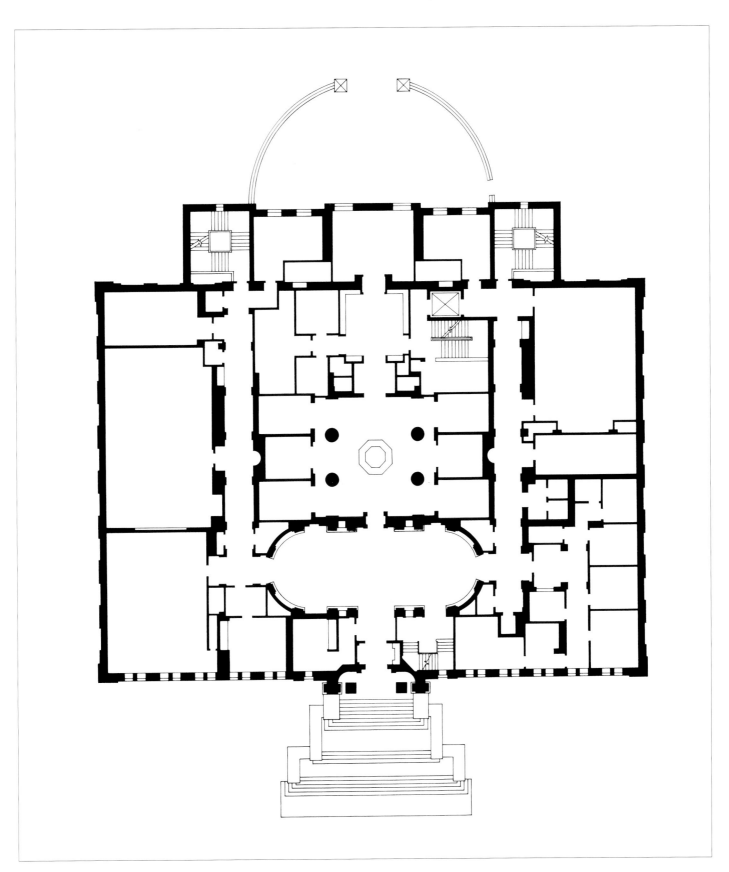

Bond Hall, Notre Dame, plan of first floor

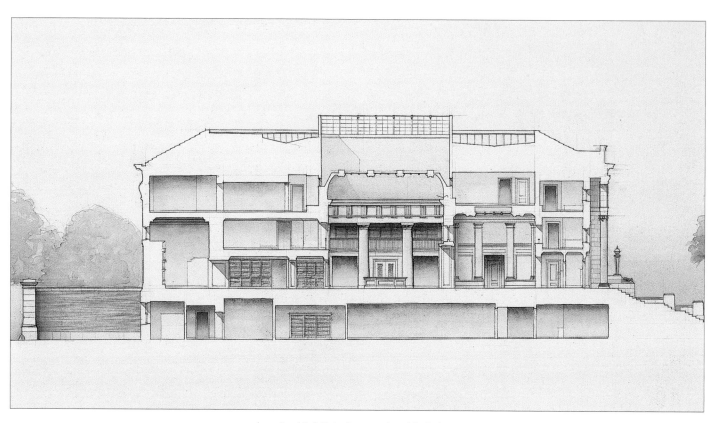

above: Bond Hall, Notre Dame, section of final scheme

below: Bond Hall, Notre Dame, elevation of 1st scheme

opposite: Bond Hall, Notre Dame, library

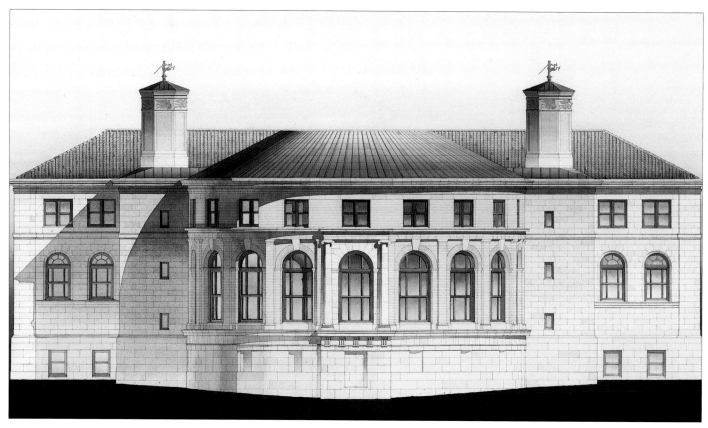

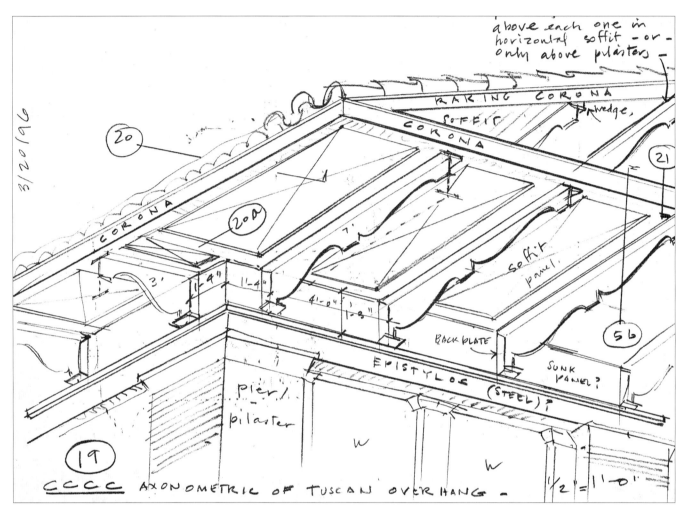

Civic Center, Cathedral City, working drawing of Tusan overhang

One of the most difficult challenges facing many American towns and cities at the end of the twentieth century is how to recover a sense of place or *genius loci*. This need is particularly felt in those settlements which have experienced their greatest growth in the post war era, where planning has been primarily for the motor car rather than the pedestrian. Smith had, of course, first-hand experience of just such a characterless place having grown up in El Cerrito, California. He therefore had a very clear idea of the problem when he was invited by MWM Architects, Inc, to collaborate with them in a competition for a new civic centre for Cathedral City, California. The Oakland firm of

MWM had in fact been his first professional employer after he graduated from Berkeley some two decades earlier. The programme brief called for a town hall with ancillary offices including a police headquarters for a desert site in the Coachella Valley.

Smith's initial scheme was an ambitious tripartite composition dominated by a three-storey central block with an octagonal lantern and a portico of free-standing Doric columns. To this the restrained end pavilions were linked by six-bay wings, along the ground floor of which ran projecting arcades. While this proposal won the competition, concerns were voiced that it was "too Italian, too Roman, too Imperial" and in addition it

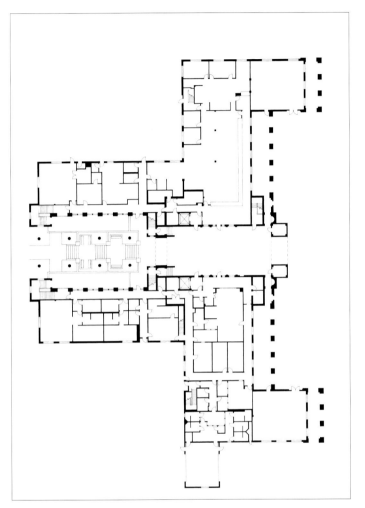

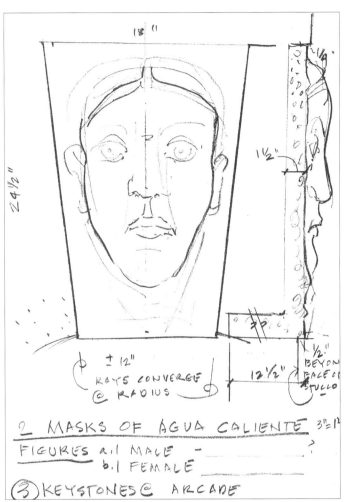

above left: Civic Center, Cathedral City, plan

above right: Civic Center, Cathedral City, working drawings of Agua Caliente mask

was emphasised that all the iconography of the building should relate to the Coachella Valley.[2] This latter request Smith was, of course, only too happy to fulfill to as it corresponded to his own belief in the ability of the classical canon to reflect regional character through the iconography of its details. A rapid design development process ensued, with Smith constantly faxing revisions to the Oakland firm in response to the City's concerns. The classical detailing of balconies featured the skulls of big horn mountain sheep instead of bucrania, in recognition of the local fauna; and the keystones of the arcade bore relief sculptures of male and female Agua Caliente Indians, the area's indigenous inhabitants. To avoid any sense of "Big Government" and to give it more of the character of the early Californian missions, all columns were eventually stripped away. As this simplification of detail occurred, it was compensated for by increasing volumetric complexity: the central block became cruciform with an octagonal upper level for the council chamber having a smaller octagonal lantern above. The main double height entrance arch is continued through the entire building as a paseo and above, a deep balcony overlooks the forecourt as a setting for civic functions. The project, costing a little over ten million dollars, was completed in mid 1998.

above: Civic Center, Cathedral City, competition elevation

below: Civic Center, Cathedral City, detail of competition perspective

opposite: Civic Center, Cathedral City, view of side pavilion

overleaf: Civic Center, Cathedral City, view of entrance from angle

Sacred Works

opposite: Cardinal Newman Institute Retreat, elevation

above: Cardinal Newman Institute Retreat, section

For Smith, the relationship between his Catholic faith and his interest in classicism had been central to his development as an architect. He attributes his initial openness to the tradition to his earliest religious instruction: "One of the reasons I felt that I was receptive as a teenager to Classicism … was the issue of knowing intuitively through Catholic upbringing that there is a great deal to be learned from the past".[3] However, while he had been brought up as a Catholic, he had drifted from the church to join a high branch of Episcopalianism; his return to the fold of Roman Catholicism took place while he was studying Baroque architecture in Rome, and therefore occurred at the same time as he seriously embraced classicism in his architecture. In the wake of his own "re-conversion", his wife also converted to Catholicism. It was this link between his religious and his architectural beliefs, in fact, which made the shift from the ironic post-modernism *of his ear*ly Californian work to a literate classicism possible during his year at the American Academy in Rome; while the oratory of St Jean Vianney was only a hypothetical project, it clearly

above: Our Lady of Guadalupe seminary, Lincoln

opposite above: Our Lady of Guadalupe seminary, perspective

opposite below: Our Lady of Guadalupe seminary, aerial perspective

opposite and above: Our Lady of Guadalupe seminary, Lincoln

Cardinal Newman Institute Retreat, sketch

belonged to a very different category to all his previous projects, which were residential, domestic and personal. In this Oratory project, Smith had for the first time to deal with the timeless verities of Christian revelation, the iconographic traditions of the Catholic church and the historical setting of the eternal city. This context required him to abandon the ironic, post-modern approach to the classical tradition and instead engage with it seriously as a living entity.

Following his "re-conversion", Smith's newly-found commitment to Catholicism ruled him out from what might have been a fascinating religious commission. Philip Johnson, the eminence grise of American architecture, designed his extraordinary Crystal Cathedral for Dr Robert Schuller, the evangelical pastor of the Garden Grove Community Church, California.[4] Three years after the building's completion in 1980 the congregation had grown to such an extent that Schuller approached the seventy-seven year old Johnson to ask if he could recommend an architect to do additional work for the church. Johnson responded in fulsome terms: "I have been thinking of a suitable architect ever since your letter arrived. The only one

with the sensitivity and I believe the dedication for you kind of work would be a young San Francisco architect named Thomas Gordon Smith ... You must meet with him to see if the chemistry would work and whether the direction his designs are taking would be pleasing to you or not. Personally, I like them very much".[5] Smith duly went for an interview with Schuller, but from the moment the question of personal religion came up it became quite clear that the "chemistry" would not work after all as Smith's Roman faith made him completely unacceptable to the church as a possible architect.

Smith is a member of the Society for Catholic Liturgy, an organisation of liturgists, theologians, historians, architects and musicians, who are assessing with concern the changes that have taken places since the Second Vatican Council. While Smith does not see an exact correspondence between architectural and liturgical changes, he admitted to being "sympathetic to the use of Latin in liturgy and feel that Latin has been stripped away in much the same way as modernists deprived us of "Latin" architecture at an earlier period."[6] An example of the problem is the

*Chapel, Domino's Pizza Headquarters, Ann Arbor,
Altar made by Robert Brandt*

philistinism encouraged by a paper publ*ished by the* Committee on the Liturgy of the National Conference of Catholic Bishops in 1978. Entitled "Environment and Art in Catholic Worship", its enthusiasm to embrace new technologies and abandon traditional iconography is apparent, for example, from its recommendation that "a new church building or renovation project should make provision for screens and/or walls which will make the projection of films, slides and filmstrips visible to the entire assembly".[7] Smith has combatted the prevalence of modernism in the Catholic church on three fronts: he has himself written forcefully against it;[8] he has encouraged student assignments for the design of new churches at the school of architecture with the support of a young faculty member he recruited to Notre Dame, Duncan Stroik; and finally, he has himself realised a number of commissions for sacred buildings with great conviction in the continuing appropriateness of the classical tradition.

The first of Smith's religious designs to be realised was rather unusual in that it was for a captain of industry, rather than a priest. Thomas Monaghan, chief executive officer of Domino's Pizza asked him to design a small chapel for their administrative headquarters in Ann Arbor, Michigan. The chapel was to be created in the basement of a conventional office building, which had the usual suspended acoustic tile ceiling and characterless fittings. To imbue the space with the sense of the sacred, Smith chose colours for the walls and ceiling that would focus attention on the liturgical fixtures he introduced: an altar, lectern and baldacchino. The forms of the altar and lectern betray Smith's study of the cabinetmaking traditions of American Greek Revival furniture and the publications of British designers such as John Taylor's *The Upholsterer's and Cabinet Maker's Pocket Assistant* (London 1825-6). A set of hanging brass lamps completes the transformation from anonymous office space to a sacred place for contemplation and worship.

The Rev. George Rutler who had helped Smith during his time in Rome by being a surrogate client became a real client in 1995. He asked Smith to develop a conceptual design for a retreat house and study centre near New York City for the Cardinal Newman Institute, where Rutler was now based. The

above: St Joseph's Church, Dalton, perspective of cloister

below: St Joseph's Church, distant perspective

above: St Joseph's Church, interior

below: St Joseph's Church, exterior view

programme was essentially for a compact monastery rather than a church, as it required a small chapel, a library and modest residential accommodation. The library was housed in a triple height octagonal space, the ground level of which would be used for meetings and seminars. The middle zone would have bookshelves on all eight sides which would be accessible from a cantilevered gallery. The vault would culminate in a tall octagonal cupola which externally was articulated like the hellenistic Tower of the Winds in the Athenian Agora. In place of the relief sculptures of the eight winds which decorated the original monument, Smith designed seven sculptural panels to represent the Offices of the day. These would be aligned according to the movement of the sun, so that the north-eastern face, which would be struck by the rising sun, featured Lauds and the north-western, which would be illuminated by the setting sun, featured Vespers. The North face, which would never be directly lit, would feature Eucharistic symbols in reference to the heavenly time of the Eighth Day. While the cupola would have a functional role, in housing the vents for the mechanical systems and accommodating a set of bells, Smith also envisaged a symbolic interpretation of it based on Matthew 5:15, "No one lights a lamp to put it under a bushel; they put it on the lampstand where it shines for everyone in the house ...", so that the octagonal tower "should be seen as a lantern on a hill to proclaim that delight in Christ has been established in a new place for a renewed time."[9] While this project clearly helped Smith understand how one might adapt pagan iconography for Christian purposes, it unfortunately did not proceed beyond the conceptual stage. A similar fate met the second commission from Thomas Monaghan, who had clearly been pleased with what Smith had achieved with an unpromising space and a modest budget in the Domino's Pizza headquarters. In 1996 he asked Smith to design a Dominican Convent for a site in Ann Arbor, Michigan, and he took the opportunity in this larger project to explore further many of the iconographic themes which had occupied him in the Cardinal Newman centre.

After disappointment in these two sacred projects, it is heartening to be able to record that, at the time of writing, Smith has two other religious commissions which are in construction: a church dedicated to St Joseph for a congregation in Dalton, Georgia, and a seminary for the Priestly Fraternity of St Peter in Lincoln, Nebraska.

The Priestly Fraternity of St Peter is a reforming Roman Catholic confraternity of priests dedicated to reviving the traditional Latin Mass. It was founded in 1988 with papal approval but, as the use of Latin is extremely controversial, the group has been welcomed in only a minority of dioceses in the United States. Although vocations have grown steadily, the fraternity's initial attempt to find a disused convent or seminary to renovate for their own use has not succeeded. This failure to find a suitable facility lead to the idea of buiding a new seminary in the diocese of Lincoln, Nebraska. Smith received the commission to design Our Lady of Guadalupe seminary in 1998 and it is expected that the first phase of the project will be completed during the Jubilee year of 2000. The complex of buildings is based on early Christian and Romanesque monastic models such as Santa Maria in Cosmedin in Rome and the hundred-acre site will be planted in an Italianate fashion with cedars and sycamores according to the designs of the landscape architect Dennis Shearer. The project is necessarily being built according to a carefully phased programme so that the first buildings to be constructed will form three sides of a quadrangle, and include accommodation for both seminarians and priests, an Aula, a library, a refectory and the administrative offices. The Aula will function as the chapel until this is built in the second phase of constuction in perhaps two years time. The seminary will be entirely constructed of load-bearing masonry with the palette of materials on the exterior ranging from limestone, for the euthynteria and details such as colonnettes flanking the main entrance, through various shades and scales of brick, to square cedar posts in the cloister. Careful thought has been given in the planning to liturgical as well as circulatory functions, allowing the seminarians to line up before Mass in the

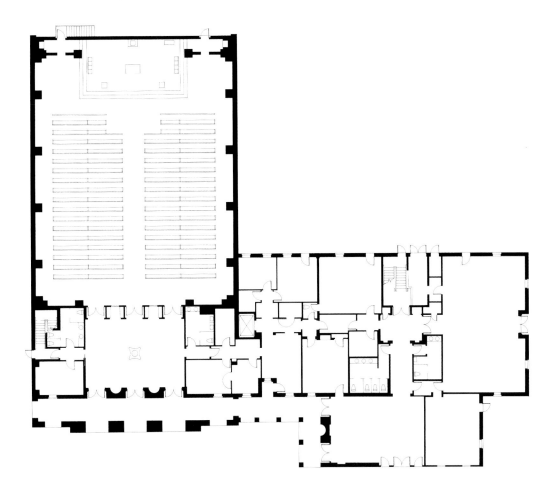

St Joseph's Church, Dalton, ground floor plan

"Statio" hall, for the Priests to process from the Sacristy into the North transept of the chapel, and after services for all to ascend the Scala Magna to the refectory. While not yet complete, the already evident success of this commission has led to another similar request, this time for a Benedictine monastery in Tulsa, Oklahoma, which is currently in the preliminary phases of the design process.

The second religious project currently in construction, is St Joseph's Church in Dalton, Georgia consisting of a church and an Aula Magna (assembly hall) linked by a wing of administrative offices and classrooms. The church community is an interesting mixture of established Americans of European descent and recent immigrants from Mexico who have been drawn to Dalton by ample opportunities for work in carpet manufacturing. In order to define an image with which both groups could identify Smith looked to counter-reformation models such as San Gregorio Magno in Rome. The result is an austere façade in brick which on account of severe cost restraints is astylar. The piers of the lower portico are determined by an unexpressed Doric trabeation onto which columns could be imposed at a later date. The seond floor has three tall arched windows supporting an Ionic entablature with pediment above and similar large arched windows also articulate the side facades. From the ground floor arcade three doors open into the narthex, below the choir loft, and from here one enters the nave directly. This simple rectangular volume is articulated by a giant order of square piers supporting a segmental vault and culminates in a large circular window above the altar. An L-shaped single-story brick cloister extends to the south-west of the church, behind which rises the Aula Magna and the two-storey wing of offices and classrooms.

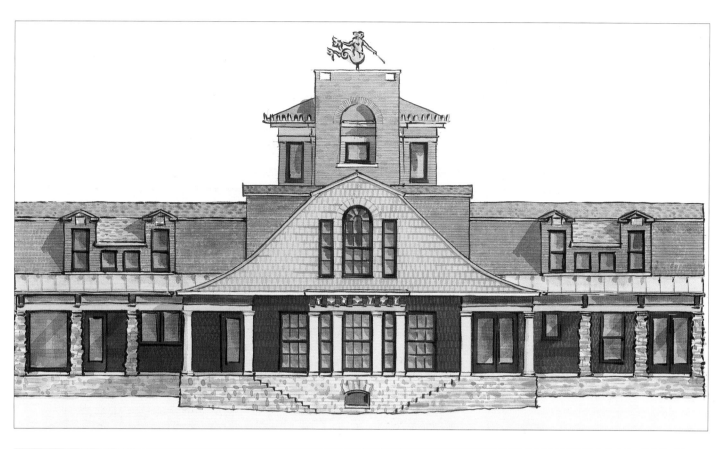

Other Works in Progress

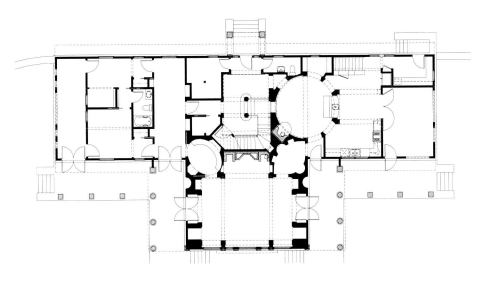

above: House, Wisconsin, plan

opposite above: House, Wisconsin, elevation

opposite below: House, Wisconsin, distant perspective

Smith has designed a country residence for a large estate in rural Wisconsin which is due to be completed in the spring of 2000. The generous budget for this 7,000 square feet house allowed him to reprise a variety of themes familiar from his early work. Here he has resurrected the Dutch American idiom which he had first explored in his scheme for the Rockwell museum. This language particularly appeals to Smith on account of its ability to accommodate a certain eclecticism in much the same way that the eighteenth century colonial version of the Dutch style continued until the 1820s and 30s exhibiting increasing hybridisation with the Anglo-federal and Grecian styles. A number of the details are drawn from an example of just such hybridisation: the Vreeland house of c.1818 in New Jersey which was published in the White Pine series in the early twentieth century. The overall composition for a site on the edge of a meadow backed by forested hills was inspired by Palladio's Villa Maser with a central block dominated by a gambrel gable and a thermal window from which two subsidiary *wing*s extend at right angles. The overall composition is anchore*d by* a three storied octagonal tower, housing an office on its top level which is reached by a spiral staircase from a library below. Smith's interest in polychromy and in complex figured spaces is given free reign in this project, with an circular dining roo*m as well a*s richly coloured elements both inside and outside. The dining room walls are covered with delft-like tiles painted with the birds of Wisconsin, to echo the framed Audubon prints which will be placed elsewhere in the house. The cruciform living room has a inglenook fireplace on its north wall, a large three light window to the south, and French windows opening on to covered porches to the East and West. Reflecting his earliest interest in Frank Lloyd Wright, the broad inglenook hearth of the living room is constructed out of the same Wisconsin sedimentary limestone, Fond du Lac, used at Taliesin and, in fact, was quarried on site. The same stone is also used externally as a basement course for the house, thus rooting the building both visually and intellectually in its location. Most unusually, however, the form of the hearth is taken from one which appears in a film beloved of both Smith and the client, George Cukor's Holiday, starring Katharine Hepburn and Cary Grant.

ENDNOTES

CHAPTER I

1 Edward Staniford, *El Cherrito: Historical Evolution*, El Cerrito 1976.

2 On Duncan see Ann Daly, *Done Into Dance: Isadora Duncan in America*, Bloomington, Indiana, 1995.

3 On Maybeck and his role in this house see Kenneth Cardwell, *Bernard Maybeck: Architect, Artisan, Artist*, Salt Lake City 1983, pp.163-4.

4 Thomas Gordon Smith, "Die Gabe des Janus", *Jahrbuch fur Architektur*, Frankfurt 1983, p.145.

5 Antonio de Bonis' interview with Paolo Portoghesi, in Charles Jencks, ed., *Free-Style Classicism*, London 1981, pp.15-16.

6 Letter from Thomas Gordon Smith to Michael Graves, no date.

7 On Esherick see Sally Woodbridge, ed., *Bay Area Houses*, Salt Lake City 1988, pp.183-195.

8 In all five commissions were received, three of which were realised: The remodelling and extension of a Hudson Thomas house damaged by fire for Michael and Shirley Issel in 1982; the remodelling, extension and addition of a carport to a Hudson Thomas house for James and Barbara Gordley in 1983; and the interior remodelling of a Dutch American style house for Thomas and Helen Barber in 1983.

9 Thomas Gordon Smith, "John Hudson Thomas", in Robert Winter, ed., *Toward a Simpler Way of Life: The Arts and Crafts Architects of California*, Berkeley and Los Angeles, 1997, pp.83-92.

10 Letter from Thomas Gordon Smith to David Gebhard, dated September 1978; Letter from David Gebhard to Thomas Gordon Smith, dated 3 October 1978.

11 David Gebhard et al., *Guide to Architecture in San Francisco and Northern California*, Salt Lake City 1985.

12 Smith, *Rule and Invention*, p.xiii.

13 *Ibid.*, p.14.

CHAPTER II

1 Smith refers to his slide collection in an undated resumé he prepared when teaching at the College of Marin, page 2.

2 Kenneth Cardwell, *Bernard Maybeck: Architect, Ertisan, Artist*, Salt Lake City 1983, p.232.

3 Thomas Gordon Smith, "Bernard Maybeck's Wallen II House", *Fine Homebuilding*, Newton, Connecticut, April/May 1981, pp.18-25.

4 Resumé prepared by Smith when teaching at the College of Marin, page 2.

5 Smith illustrated both in *Rule and Invention*: the Maybeck House p.6; the Villa delle Torre at Fumane, p.67.

6 For instance, Mies' Tugendhat House, Brno, Czechoslovakia of 1928-30.

7 Christian Norberg-Schulz, *Kilian Ignaz Dientzenhofer e il barocco boemo*, Rome 1968.

8 Letter from Christian Norberg-Schulz to Thomas Gordon Smith, dated 10 June 1978.

9 For an account of the development of this evolutionary tree see Charles Jencks, *Architecture 2000*, London 1971, pp.35-48.

10 Letter to Charles Jencks from Thomas Gordon Smith, dated 7 October 1977.

11 Inscription by Richard Long on a drawing dated 8 February 1979.

12 Letter to Charles Jencks from Thomas Gordon Smith, dated 12 March 1978.

13 The tradition of phallic plans stretches back at least to the eighteenth century; in addition to Claude Nicolas Ledoux's famous Oikéma, Sir John Soane designed a mausoleum for the Earl of Chatham in 1779 in this form, see David Watkin, *Sir John Soane: Enlightenment Thought and the Royal Academy Lectures*, Cambridge 1996, p.222; for the Ledoux see *Architecture de C.N. Ledoux*, Paris 1847, plate 240.

14 Arthur Dexler, *The Architecture of the Ecole des Beaux Arts*, New York 1977.

15 For a detailed description of how the house was constructed see Thomas Gordon Smith, "Bernard Maybeck's Wallen II House", *Fine Homebuilding*, Newton, Connecticut, April/May 1981, pp.18-25.

16 On Loviot and his *envoi* of the Parthenon see Ecole Nationale Supérieure des Beaux-Arts, *Paris Rome Athens: Travels in Greece by French Architects in the Nineteenth and Twentieth Centuries*, Houston, Texas, 1982, pp.230-37.

17 Smith, *Rule and Invention*, p.113.

18 Thomas Gordon Smith, "Re-drawing from Classicism", *Journal of Architectural Education*, Vol.XXXII, No1, September 1978, p.18.

19 Letter to Charles Jencks from Thomas Gordon Smith, 6 March 1979.

20 On this tradition see Pierre de la Ruffinière du Prey, *The Villas of Pliny from Antiquity to Posterity*, Chicago 1994.

21 For the plan of this house see Peter Arnell and Ted Bickford, ed., *Robert A.M. Stern 1965-1980: Toward a Modern Architecture after Modernism*, New York 1981, p.62.

22 "Three examples of post-modern classicism", *House and Garden*, December 1982, pp.108-9; "Palladio in America", *House Beautiful*, January 1983, p.65.

CHAPTER III

1 Letter from Thomas Gordon Smith to Charles Moore, dated 16 February 1979.

2 The interior is illustrated in Kevin P. Keim, *An Architectural Life: Memoirs and Memories of Charles W. Moore*, Boston 1996, p.175.

3 Joseph Connors, *Borromini and the Roman Oratory*, Cambridge 1980.

4 This research was subsequently published as John Beldon Scott, *Images of Nepotism: The Painted Ceilings of the Palazzo Barberini*, Princeton 1991.

5 See the catalogue of the exhibition: *The Presence of the Past*, Venice 1980.

6 Two obvious exceptions were the facades by Léon Krier and Allan Greenberg.

7 Smith, *Rule and Invention*, pp.20-23.

8 Letter from James Ackerman to Thomas Gordon Smith, no date.

9 Charles Jencks, *Free-Style Classicism*, London 1981, p.7.

10 For this method see Andrea Pozzo, *Rules and Examples of Perspective Proper for Painters and Architects*, fascimile of 1707 translation by John James, New York, 1971, plate LIIB.

11 Vincent Scully, "How things got to be the way they are now", *The Presence of the Past*, Venice 1980.

CHAPTER IV

1 Letter from Marika Wilson Smith to John Beldon Scott, dated 28 October 1980.

2 Letter from Thomas Gordon Smith to John Beldon Scott, dated 21 September 1983.

3 Euripides, *Iphigenia in Tauris*, 112f.

CHAPTER V

1 Benjamin Clavan, "The Challenge of Finding Just Plain Good Architecture", *San Francisco Bay Architects' Review*, June/July 1979, p.1.

2 Carl Davis, "The Challenge of Exterior Decoration", *San Francisco Bay Architects' Review*, June/July 1979, p.5.

3 Smith had become personally involved in Baroque opera some time earlier, as he had designed and painted movable sets for the U.C. Berkeley's production of *Armide* in 1982.

4 Letter from Lother Haselberger to Thomas Gordon Smith, dated 17 May 1987.

5 Monacelli Press, 1999.

6 David Greenspan, "An Interview with Stanley Tigerman", *Inland Architect*, September-October 1989.

7 For and account of this phenomenon see P.H. Scholfield, *The Theory of Proportion in Architecture*, Cambridge 1958, especially chapters III and IV.

8 Letter from Jerome Pollitt to Thomas Gordon Smith, dated 2 March 1986.

9 "Stanley Tigerman comments on UIC School of Architecture after five years as Director", *The University of Illinois at Chicago School of Architecture Newsletter*, Spring 1990.

10 Thomas King, *Neo-Classical Furniture Designs: A Reprint of Thomas King's "Modern Style of Cabinet Work Exemplified", 1829*, New York, 1995, p.xiv.

11 *John Hall and the Grecian Style in America*, New York 1996.

12 Thomas Gordon Smith "Millford Plantation in South Carolina", *The Magazine Antiques*, May 1997.

CHAPTER VI

1 For this incident see Cassius Dio, book 69.

2 Dan Weeks, "Building the Country House, *Country Home*, October 1995, p.66.

3 *Ibid.*, p.72.

CHAPTER VII

1 Letter from Heinrich Klotz to Thomas Gordon Smith, dates 1 March 1988.

2 Letter from Robert Wood of MWM Architects, Inc., to Thomas Gordon Smith, dated 28 March 1996.

3 Quoted by Ann Carey in her "Ever Ancient, Ever New", *Sursum Corda!*, Vol.3, No.1, Winter 1998, p.7.

4 For a recent account of Philip Johnson's impact on the course of American architecture see Franz Schulze, *Philip Johnson: Life and Work*, New York 1994.

5 Letter from Philip Johnson to Robert Schuller, dated 19 October 1983.

6 "Interview: Thomas Gordon Smith on the 'New Classicism'", *Antiphon: Publication of the Society for Catholic Liturgy*, Vol.2 No.1, Spring 1997, p.10.

7 Quoted by Jeffrey Rubin in his "Traditional Church Architecture for the 21st Century", *The Latin Mass – Special Edition*, p.10.

8 Thomas Gordon Smith, "A New Architecture to Honor The Church's Vision and Legacy", *Catholic Dossier*, May-June 1997, Vol.3, No.3, pp.27-30.

9 *Ibid*, p.30.

BIBLIOGRAPHY

Allen, Gerald, "A Guide to Architect Designed Houses", *Town and Country*, New York, October 1979.

Allende, Gabriel, "Two Houses", *Arquitectura*, Madrid, September/October 1979, p. 27.

Bagdonas, Charlotte M., "El Greco's Assumption: Thomas Gordon Smith's new frame for an Art Institute masterpiece", *The Chicago Architecture Annual*, 1987, p. 15.

Bergdoll, Barry., "Prototypes and archetypes: Deutsches Architekturmuseum, Frankfurt, Germany", *Architectural Record*, August 1984, pp 104-117.

Blodgett, Bonnie, "Design: A Home with Heart", *TWA Ambassador*, October 1985, p. 116.

Bolz, Diane M., "Smithsonian Highlights: A panorama of design history", *Smithsonian*, December 1991, pp 133-137.

Bortolon, Liana, "L'architettura inventa il passato", *Grazia*, V. 53, No.2063, July 9, 1980, pp 34-36.

Bottero, Maria, "Il Postmodernism alla Biennale di Venezia" *Abitare*, Milan, November 1980, pp 106-110.

Branch, Mark Alden, "Going for Baroque", *Progressive Architecture*, September 1988, v. 69, No. 9, p. 133.

Brenner, D., "Grove House, San Diego County, California", *Architectural Record*, April 1986, No. 174, pp 104-109.

Brown, Patricia Leigh Brown, "Architecture's Young Old Fogies", *New York Times*; February, 9, 1995; reprinted in *US Air Magazine*, September 1995.

California: E.O. Moss, Morphosis, etc, "California Architects", *Space Design*, August 1982, No. 215, pp 4-13, 15-31.

Carey, Ann, "Passion for the Classical Perspective: At Notre Dame's School of Architecture Classicism and Catholicism Run Along Parallel Lines", *Our Sunday Visitor*, August 24, 1997, pp 1, 10-11.

Carey, Ann, "Ever Ancient, Ever New", *Sursum Corda!*, Fort Collins, Colorado, Winter 1998, pp 6-10.

Claven, Benjamin, "The Perils of Post Modernism", *San Francisco Bay Architects Review*, June/July 1979, pp 1,2.

Cleary, Richard, "Design and Designers: Book Reviews", *Design Book Review*, Spring 1991, pp 72-73.

Culot, Maurice, "Les Ordres de Thomas Gordon Smith", *Archives d'Architecture Moderne*, Bruxelles; November 1977.

D'Arms, John H., Editor, "Thomas Gordon Smith", *Annual Exhibition of the American Academy in Rome 1980*, catalogue.

Davis, Carl, "The Challenge of Exterior Decoration", *San Francisco Bay Architects Review*, June/July 1979, p.5.

Davis, Douglas, "Designs for Living", *Newsweek*, November 6, 1978, pp 85,89.

Du Prey, Pierre de la Ruffiniere, *The Villas of Pliny from Antiquity to Posterity*, University of Chicago Press, 1994, pp 31-32.

Field, John Louis , "A Critique of the Biennale Show", *San Francisco Bay Architects' Review*, Summer 1982, pp 2, 23.

Fillip, Janice, "A Review of The California Condition", *Architecture California*, November/December 1982, V. 4, No 6, pp 14-21.

Fujii, Wayne N. T., "Tuscan House and Laurentian House", *Global Architecture*, Tokyo; 1982.

Fujii, Wayne N. T., "New Waves in American Architecture", *Special Issue Global Architecture Houses*, March 1982, No. 10, pp 40-175.

Galinsky, Karl, *Classical and Modern Interactions: Postmodern Architecture, Multiculturalism, Decline and Other Issues*, University of Texas Press, Austin 1992, pp 11-13.

Gebhard, David and Susan King, *A View of California Architecture*, Catalogue for exhibitions at the San Francisco Museum of Modern Art, the Santa Barbara Museum of Modern Art, and the La Jolla Museum; 1976; pp 7,12,44,61.

Gebhard, David, Eric Sandweiss, and Robert Winter, *Architecture in San Francisco and Northern California*, Peregrine Smith Books, Salt Lake City1985; Cover photograph and pp 241, 322.

Giovannini, Joseph, "Re-using Architectural Artifacts: The Old is New Again", *The New York Times*, June 6, 1985, pp C1, C6.

Giovannini, Joseph, "After the White Wall: Elaborately Painted Rooms", *The New York Times*, June 20, 1985, p. C1.

Goldberger, Paul, "Saving a Museum's Beaux-Arts Past...", *New York Times*, August 16, 1987, pp 29-30.

Goldberger, Paul, "Back to the Past", *The New Republic*, November 27, 1995, pp 42-45.

Greenberg, Allan with Philip Langdon, "Classic Buildings in a Modern Age", *The American Enterprise*, Washington DC, March/April, 1997, p.57.

Greenspan, David, "An Interview with Stanley Tigerman", *Inland*

Architect, September/October 1987.

Gregory, Daniel P., "Radical Palladianism", *Concrete*, The College of Environmental Design, U.C. Berkeley, Summer 1978, p. 6.

Gregory, Daniel P., "Precocious Houses: Four Recent Works by Bay Area Architects", *Precocious Houses*, Exhibition catalogue, The Oakland Museum, Oakland, California June 1985.

Haker, Werner, "Neve Tendenzen in den USA", *Werk, Bauen + Wohnen*, No 5, Zurhich, May 1992, pp 12-13.

Harling, Robert, "Inspired by Pliny", *House & Garden*, London, December 1982, pp 108-109.

Jencks, Charles, *The Language of Post-Modern Architecture*, Rizzoli, New York 1977, p. 132.

Jencks, Charles, "A Genealogy of Post-Modern Architecture", *Architectural Design*, London, No. 4, 1977, pp 269-271.

Jencks, Charles, "Post Modern History", *Architectural Design*, London, no. 1, 1978, p. 57.

Jencks, Charles, "Late Modernism and Post Modernism", *Architectural Design*, London 1978, V. 48, No. 1, pp 593-609.

Jencks, Charles, "What is Post-Modern Architecture?", *Progressive Architecture*, April 1978, pp 10-12.

Jencks, Charles, "Tuscan House and Laurentian House" *Post-Modern Classicism: The New Synthesis*, Architectural Design, London 1980, pp 48-52.

Jencks, Charles, "Free-Style Classicism", *Architectural Design*, No 1-2, London, 1982, pp 1-145.

Jencks, Charles, *Current Architecture*, Rizzoli, New York; 1982.

Jencks, Charles, *Post-Modernism: The New Classicism in Art and Architecture*, Academy Editions, London 1987, pp 222, 223, 302-305.

Jensen, Robert and Patricia Conway, *Ornamentalism: The New Decorativeness in Architecture and Design*, Crown, New York; 1982.

Kahn, Eve, "The New Classicists: A Portfolio of Contemporary Designs in the Classical Tradition", *Traditional Building*, November/December 1990, p. 6.

Kahn, Eve, "Thomas Gordon Smith: The man who is bringing Classicism Out of Exile", *Traditional Building*, March/April 1993, pp 6-7, 72-73.

King, Carol Soucek, "The Presence of the Past", Designers West, No 5; 1982, pp 89-92.

Klotz, Heinrich, "Das 'Laurentianische' und das 'Tuskische' Haus", *Jahrbuch fur Architektur 1982*, Deutsches Architekturmuseum, Frankfurt 1982, pp 188-199.

Klotz, Heinrich, *The History of Post-Modern Architecture*, M.I.T. Press, Cambridge, Massachusetts, 1988, p. 433.

Klotz, Heinrich, *Moderne und Postmoderne: Architektur der Gegenwart 1960-1980*, Friedr. Vieweg & Sohn, Braunschweig/Wiesbaden, 1984, pp 202, 206-210.

Klotz, Heinrich, *Postmodern Visions: Drawings, Paintings and Models by Contemporary Architects*, Abbeville Press, New York, 1985, pp 263-278.

Knox, Marion, et al. "America - America", *Bauwelt*, V. 89, No. 112, January 8, 1982, pp 16-55.

Koster, Baldur, *Palladio in Amerika: Die Continuitat klassizistischen Bauens in den USA*, Prestel Verlag, 1990, p. 131.

Kulterman, Udo, "Space, Time and the New Architecture", *Architecture and Urbanism*, Tokyo, February 1981, pp 14,15,29.

Labine, Clem, "Rumblings from the Classical Crypt", *Traditional Building*, March/April 1993, pp 4, 70-73.

Laine, Christian, "Books: Classical Architecture: Rule and Invention", *Metropolitan Review*, July/August 1988, p. 22.

Lavvas, George P., "Classicism, Historicism, Eclecticism", *The Neoclassical City and Architecture*, Thessaloniki, 1983.

LeBlanc, Doug, "Make Room for Dada", *Christianity Today*, February 5, 1990, p. 69.

Lewin, Susan, "Palladio in America", *House Beautiful*, New York, January 1983, p. 65.

Lovejoy, Diane Planer, "The Assumption of the Virgin", *The Art Institute of Chicago News & Events*, Chicago, 1989, p. 7 and cover photograph of frame by Thomas Gordon Smith.

Malone, Maggie, "Il Kitsch fatto in casa", *l'altro Panorama*, 1982, pp 16-17.

Mannion, Frances, "Interview with Thomas Gordon Smith on the 'New Classicism'", *Antiphon*, Spring 1997, pp 8-11.

Meccoli, Sandro, "All'Arsenale di Venezia fiorisce l'architettura", *Corriere della Sera Illustrato*; August 2, 1980, pp 16-18.

Monczunski, John, "Edifice Rex", *Notre Dame Magazine*, Notre Dame, Indiana, Winter; 1990-91, pp 43-48.

Monczunski, John, "A Classical Solution", *Notre Dame Magazine*, Notre Dame, Indiana, Summer 1996, pp 32-41.

Monczunski, John, "Something Old, Something New", *Notre Dame Magazine*, Spring 1997.

Monczunski, John, "Athens, Indiana: 46656", *Notre Dame Magazine*, Notre Dame, Indiana, Summer 1996, pp 36-37.

Morton, David, "Eclectic Revivals", *Progressive Architecture*, Stamford, Connecticut, October 1981, pp 98-101.

Meyer-Wieser, "Grey Architecture", *Werk Bauen + Wohnen*, No 5, Zurich, May 1982, pp 75, 89.

Nakamura, Toshio, "Thomas Gordon Smith: Five Projects", *Architecture and Urbanism*, Tokyo, February 1979, pp 7-14.

Nielsen, Hans Peter Svendler, "Mod en billedrig og Pluralistisk arkitektur" *Huset Som Billede*; Catalogue for exhibition at Lousiana Museum of Art, Copenhagen, October 1981, pp 98-101.

Ott, Ernestine, "Architects 'steal' art show in Rome", *Ashland Daily Independent*, Ashland, Oregon, June 29, 1980.

Owens, Mitchell, "Building Grace into a House", *The New York Times*, September 12, 1996.

Papadakis, Andreas and James Steele, *Classical Modern Architecture*, Terrail, London 1997, pp 129-134.

Parks, Janet, *Contemporary Architectural Drawings*, Avery Architectural and Fine Arts Library, Pomegranate Artbooks, San Francisco, l991, p. 115.

Pastier, John, et al., "Post-Modernism: The Uses of History", *Arts + Architecture*, July 1985, V. 4, No 2, pp 49-89, 94-97.

Portoghesi, Paolo, *After Modern Architecture*, Rizzoli, New York 1982, pp 75, 89.

Radice, Barbara and Maddalena Sisto, "Il Ritorno delle Colonne", *Casa Vogue*, Milan, November 1980, pp 222-226.

Richardson, Sara S., "Thomas Gordon Smith: A Bibliography", *Architecture Series: Bibliography*, Vance Bibliographies, Monticello, Illinois, January 1989.

Robinson, Cynthia, "The New Centurions: Classical Architecture is Back- Just in Time for the Second Millennium", *Homes & Ideas*, Issue 2, 1992, pp 26-28.

Rubin, Jeffrey, "Something Traditional at Notre Dame: Traditional Church Architecture for the 21st Century", *Latin Mass Magazine*, May-June 1994, pp 12-19.

Scheiman, Diane, "Modern Design: The Influence of Palladio", *Design Lines*, V. 4, No 1, Winter 1986, pp 1, 8.

Schwarz, Hans-Peter, Zwischen individueller Pragmatik und professioneller Utopie: Das Architektenhaus der Gegenwart, pp 164-168.

Scott, Cynthia, "Thomas Gordon Smith: Teaching Architects the Poetry of Their Craft", *Notre Dame*, Notre Dame; October 1991.

Scully, Vincent, "How Things Got to be the Way They are Now", *The Presence of the Past*, Catalogue for La Biennale di Venezia, Electa Editrice, Milan, 1980, p. 18.

Scully, Vincent, *American Architecture and Urbanism*, Henry Hold and Company, New York, 1988, p. 268.

Searing, Helen, *Speaking a New Classicism: American Architecture Now*, Smith College Museum of Art catalogue of exhibition, Northampton, Massachusetts, 1981, pp 48-50.

Shay, James, *New Architecture San Francisco*, Chronicle Books, San Francisco; 1989, pp 118-121.

Silverstein, Wendy, "Designers' Sketchbook: Architectural Ornaments", *Home Magazine*, Los Angeles; December 1986, p. 74.

Sisto, Maddalena, "Domus Nova in California" *Casa Vogue*, Milan, October 1981, pp 226-229.

Skude, A. Flemming, "Amerikanske impulser 1976-1981", *Arkitekten*, V. 84, November 1982, pp 445-449.

Smith, Joan, "A Roman Palace in Richmond: Classical or Kitsch?", *Image, The San Francisco Examiner*; September 18, 1988, pp 22-26 and cover photograph.

Smith, Thomas Gordon, "Re-drawing from Classicism", *Journal of Architectural Education*, Washington DC; September 1978, pp 17-23.

Smith, Thomas Gordon, "Statement", *The Presence of the Past*: Catalogue for the Venice Biennale, Electa Editrice, Milan; 1980, pp 285-288.

Smith, Thomas Gordon, "Subject in Architecture", *San Francisco Bay Architects' Review*, Winter 1981, pp 10-12.

Smith, Thomas Gordon, "Bernard Maybeck's Wallen II House" *Fine Homebuilding Magazine*, Newtown, Connecticut; April-May 1981; pp 18-25.

Smith, Thomas Gordon, "Borromini's Rome: A Review of Borromini and the Roman Oratory" by Joseph Connors, *Progressive Architecture Stamford*, Connecticut; May 1981, pp 188, 195, 200.

Smith, Thomas Gordon, "Tuscan House and Laurentian House", *Architecture and Urbanism*, June 1981, No 129, pp 41-50.

Smith, Thomas Gordon, "Die Gabe des Janus" *Jahrbuch fur Architektur*, 1983; Deutches Architekturmuseum, Frankfurt, 1983, pp 145-150.

Smith, Thomas Gordon, "Book Reviews: La Laurentine et L'invention de la villa Romaine and Pompeii", *Design Book Review*, Berkeley, 1983, pp 30-33.

Smith, Thomas Gordon, "Book Reviews: Robert Stern and Robert A. M. Stern: Buildings and Projects 1965-1980", *Design Book Review*, Berkeley, Winter 1983, pp 28-29.

Smith, Thomas Gordon, "Book Review: The Palladians and the Great Perspectivists", *Design Book Review*, Berkeley, Winter 1983, pp 17-19.

Smith, Thomas Gordon, "Richmond Hill House", *Oz Magazine*, Kansas State University, Volume 3, 1983, pp 36-37.

Smith, Thomas Gordon, "San Francisco Architectural Club", *Concrete*: Journal of the College of Environmental Design, U.C. Berkeley, V. 28, No 1, October 1984, p. 5.

Smith, Thomas Gordon, "Architect: Thomas Gordon Smith", *Global Architect Houses*, February 1985, No. 17, pp 18-23.

Smith, Thomas Gordon, "Rule and Invention: Classical Architecture", *Arts + Architecture*, July 1985, V. 4, No 2, pp 64-69.

Smith, Thomas Gordon, "Subject Matter and Design", *Faith and Form*, Fall 1985, V. 19, pp 38-41.

Smith, Thomas Gordon, "Regula and Invenzione", *Threshold*: The Journal of the University of Illinois, Chicago, 1986.

Smith, Thomas Gordon, "The Monroe House", *The Chicago Architecture Annual*, 1987, pp 252-253.

Smith, Thomas Gordon, *Classical Architecture: Rule and Invention*, Gibbs M. Smith, Salt Lake City, 1988.

Smith, Thomas Gordon, "Habitations of the Spirit", *Image: A Journal of the Arts & Religion*, Front Royal, Virginia, Spring 1989, pp 65-74.

Smith, Thomas Gordon, "Thomas Gordon Smith", *Architectural Digest: The AD 100 Architects*, August 15, 1991, pp 216-217.

Smith, Thomas Gordon, "Vitruvian House", *Architecture and Urbanism*, No. 264, Tokyo, September 1992, pp 90-97.

Smith, Thomas Gordon, ed., *The Cabinet Maker's Assistant*, John Hall; Acanthus Press, New York; 1996.

Smith, Thomas Gordon, ed., *The Modern Style of Cabinet Work Exemplified*, Thomas King; Dover Publications, New York; 1995.

Smith, Thomas Gordon, ed., *The Builder's Guide*, Asher Benjamin; Da Capo Press, New York; 1994.

Smith, Thomas Gordon, "A New Architecture to Honor the Church's Vision and Legacy", *Catholic Dossier*, Vol. 3, No. 3, San Francisco, May-June 1997, pp 27-30. Reprinted in: *American Arts Quarterly*, Summer 1997, pp 8-12.

Smith, Thomas Gordon, "Millford Plantation", *The Magazine Antiques*; New York; May 1997.

Smith, Thomas Gordon, "John Hudson Thomas", in *Toward a Simpler Way of Life: The Arts & Crafts Architects of California*; edited by Robert Winter, University of California Press, Berkeley 1997.

Smith, Thomas Gordon, "Anthony G. Quervelle at Rosedown in Louisiana", *The Magazine Antiques*, May 2001.

Smith, Thomas Gordon, "Eternal Architecture: In Ancient Rome, Vitruvius Kept Alive the Classical Ideal", *Archaeology Odyssey Magazine*, May/June 2000, pp. 44-61.

Smith, Thomas Gordon, "Triumphs of the Classical Legacy", *Latin Mass Magazine*, Fall 1999, pp.94-104.

Smith, Thomas Gordon, "Triumphs of the Gothic Tradition", *Latin Mass Magazine*, Winter 2000, pp. 99-110.

Taylor, Henrika, "Religious Buildings: Saint Joseph Catholic Church in Dalton, Georgia", *Traditional Building Magazine*, January/February 2001, p. 16.

Kahn, Eve, "Architecture Books With the Heft of Blocks and Bricks", *The New York Times*, February 8, 2001, p. B13.

Ledes, Allison Eckardt, "Current and coming: Neoclassical Architecture", *The Magazine Antiques*, October, 2000, pp. 420-422.

Solomon, Richard, "Born Again", *Inland Architect*, Chicago, January/February 1992, pp 33-35.

Stamper, John W., "The Critics of Classicism", *The Classicist*, No 4, 1997, pp 17-23.

Stamper, John W., "Rome and the American Schools of Architecture: The University of Notre Dame", *Metamorfosi*, Rome; No 24; 1996.

Stern, Robert A. M. and Deborah Nevins, *The Architect's Eye*, Pantheon Books, New York; 1980.

Stern, Robert A. M., "American Architecture after Modernism", *Special Issue, Architecture and Urbanism*, No 3 supplement, March 1982. pp 298-304.

Stern, Robert A. M., "Las Duplicidades del Post Modernismo", *Architectura*, Madrid, September/October 1982, p. 69.

Stern, Robert A. M. with Raymond W. Gastil, *Modern Classicism*, Rizzoli, New York, pp 234-237, 246, 248; 1988.

Takeyama, Minoru, "Tuscan House and Laurentian House", *Architecture and Urbanism*, Tokyo, June 1981, pp 40-50.

Takeyama, Minoru, "Contemporary Houses of the World", *Architecture and Urbanism*, February 1979, No. 2(101), pp 7-170.

Tigerman, Stanley and Susan Lewin, *The California Condition*, La Jolla Museum of Contemporary Art, November 1982, pp 83-86.

Viladas, Pilar, "Vitruvius in Indiana", *House and Garden*, August 1992, pp 84-89.

Vidler, Anthony, "Cooking up the Classics", *Skyline: The Architecture and Design Review*, October 1981, pp18-21.

Weeks, Daniel, "Housewright: Building the Country House", *Country Home Magazine*, first article in a series chronicling the design and construction of a house by Thomas Gordon Smith; Des Moines, Iowa, October 1995, pp 65-72.

Weeks, Daniel, "Housewright: Designing the Country House", *Country Home Magazine*, December 1995, pp 66-68.

Weeks, Daniel, "Housewright: Roll Over, Vitruvius", *Country Home Magazine*, February 1996, pp 50-51.

Weeks, Daniel, "Housewright: Engineering the Country House", *Country Home Magazine*, March/April 1996, pp 74-77.

Weeks, Daniel, "Housewright: Scheduling the Job", *Country Home Magazine*, May/June 1996. p. 78.

Weeks, Daniel, "Housewright: Raising the Frame", *Country Home Magazine*, July/August 1996, pp 76-78.

Weeks, Daniel, "Housewright: Balancing Act", *Country Home Magazine*, September/October 1996, p. 122.

Weeks, Daniel, "Housewright: Country Classic", *Country Home Magazine*, February 1997, pp 104-112.

Werner, Frank, *Klassizismen und Klassiker, Tendenzen neuer europaischer Gengenwartsarchitektur*, Badischer Kunstverein, Karlsruhe, 1985, pp 45-46.

Woodbridge, Sally, "Changing Subject Matter in Bay Area Architecture", *San Francisco Bay Architects Review*, Winter 1981, p. 20.

Woodbridge, Sally, "Vestpocket Villa: Thomas Gordon Smith House, Richmond, California", *Progressive Architecture*, March 1985, V. 66, No. 3, pp 86-90.

Woodbridge, Sally, *Bay Area Houses*, Peregrine Smith Books, Salt Lake City, 1988, pp 334, 336-340.

Wu, Mingyi, "World Trade Tower", *Eastern Air Connections*, Hong Kong, June 1995, pp 48-49.

CREDITS

PHOTO CREDITS

Cover: Wolfgang Simon

page 7:   Henry Bowles

page 8:   University of Notre Dame

page 10:   O.Q. Braun

page 12:   Patricia Braybant

page 34:   Douglas Symes

page 35:   Douglas Symes

page 81:   University of Notre Dame

page 108:   Richard Pare

PROJECT CREDIT

Kulb House: Jason Montgomery and Michael Mesco

Bond Hall: Jason Montgomery and Michael Mesco

Johnson House: Thomas Marano

St Joseph's Catholic Church: William Heyer, Frank Fu-Jen Yang, Thomas Marano, Dean B. Lee

Our Lady of Guadalupe Seminary: William Heyer, Dean B. Lee, Carmine Carapella, Thomas Marano, John Mead